HOW
— *to* —
FINISH
—*the*—
CHRISTIAN
—*life*—

Following Jesus in the Second Half

DONALD W. SWEETING
& GEORGE SWEETING

MOODY PUBLISHERS
CHICAGO

Edited by Andy Scheer
Interior design: Ragont Design

Cover design: Kathryn Joachim
Illustration Credit: iStock © hypergon 2007

Library of Congress Cataloging-in-Publication Data

Sweeting, Donald W.
    How to finish the Christian life : following Jesus in the second half / Don Sweeting and George Sweeting.
        p. cm.
    Includes bibliographical references.
    ISBN 978-0-8024-3588-0
    1. Retirees—Religious life. 2. Retirement—Religious aspects—Christianity.
    I. Sweeting, George, 1924- II. Title.
    BV4596.R47S94 2012
    248.8'5—dc23

                            2011046167

We hope you enjoy this book from Moody Publishers. Our goal is to provide high-quality, thought-provoking books and products that connect truth to your real needs and challenges. For more information on other books and products written and produced from a biblical perspective, go to www.moodypublishers.com or write to:

Moody Publishers
820 N. LaSalle Boulevard
Chicago, IL 60610

5 7 9 10 8 6

Printed in the United States of America

CONTENTS

ACKNOWLEDGMENTS

THANKS:

To Bill Armstrong and my (Don's) friends at Colorado Christian University, for letting me hole up in an office during part of July to write the first half of this.

To Bob and Kim Feehs for also giving me a lovely place to write the second half.

To Christina and Margaret for their constant encouragement and support.

INTRODUCTION

THIS IS A BOOK ABOUT being a disciple of Jesus in the second half of life—and finishing in faith.

One never knows how long the second half will be. If you live in the United States, the life expectancy figure for 2011 was 78.3 years, although the United States is not at the top of the world life expectancy list. Monaco leads the list at 89.7 years. On the other end is Angola, Africa, at 38.7 years.[1] According to the UN, the average life expectancy for the world is 67.2 years.[2]

Generally speaking, we're thinking of a readership aged 40 and above. For those born before 1938, the "normal" age of retirement has been 65. For those born after 1938, it is 67. And with Social Security running out of money, who knows what it will be tomorrow. But for those within fifteen years of the "normal" retirement years, there is a lot of life reassessment going on. So let's pose a question: How do we follow Jesus through this second half of life until the day that we die?

There are lots of books about beginning the Christian life. Evangelicals have specialized in this subject. There are also a few good books on dying or "ending well." Our interest is broader. We seek to offer a Christ-centered vision for the second half of our lives. How do we go through the final part of life, faith intact, as a committed follower of Jesus? The way we end our discipleship journey is just as important as the way we begin.

THE SEED FOR THIS BOOK

The seed for this book came from a conversation between two Christian leaders—a father and a son. Some years back the father had written a popular book titled *How to Begin the Christian Life.* He followed it with another book called *How to Continue the Christian Life.* As the father, George, reached his 80s, his son Don asked him, "Dad, how about writing one last book?"

"Not interested," he said. "It's too much work, and I don't have the energy I used to."

"Look, Dad," the son said, "most writers stop writing in their seventies. A few keep going beyond that, but not many. And precious few share their unique life wisdom from that vantage point. You have something to say."

The father then gave a second excuse. "I've already written a book called *The Joys of Successful Aging.*"

"But, Dad," his impertinent son said, "that book was a little too self-helpish and unrealistic for many of us. How about going beyond that . . . with a more realistic book on spiritual formation for the second half of life? How about finishing your trilogy with a book on how to finish the Christian life?"

The son went on. "Most of us know how to begin. We also know something about continuing. But there's a whole swelling generation approaching the retirement years who want to know something about how to make it through the second half."

As I (Don) write, the baby boom generation is moving into retirement at an astonishing speed.

For the next twenty years, some ten thousand boomers a day will turn age 65. There are seventy-nine million of them. And people are generally living longer. America is graying. So thinking wisely about ending well is important. Thinking wisely about ending well as a Christian is even more important.

The father then gave a third excuse. "I am not interested in writing it. I do not carry around a laptop everywhere like you do. I don't even use a computer."

"Problem solved," the son said. "How about if I write it? Let's first have a long conversation about some of the key issues involved in being a faithful disciple of Jesus in the second half of life, and you share some of the lessons you have learned. Give me your thoughts, Dad. You have all this experience. Let's talk about these things together, blend our pastoral observations, and then I will write up the notes of our conversation."

Finally, he relented. He did so not simply out of exasperation. I could now hear interest in his voice. He knew I was on to an important topic; one that even he was wrestling with as he was living out his eighth decade. And so this book was born.

THE AUTHORS

Let me tell you a bit about the authors. It is another thing that makes this book unique.

George Sweeting is 87 years old. He has been an evangelist, pastor, author, and educator. He pastored churches in New Jersey and Illinois. The last church he served as senior pastor was the Moody Church in Chicago. He's currently serving part-time on the pastoral staff of a church in Lake Villa, Illinois, which the son helped plant.

Don Sweeting, now in his 50s, is George's third son. He's been a pastor for twenty-two years. He served as founding pastor of the Chain of Lakes Community Bible Church in Lake Villa, Illinois. After that, he was senior pastor of Cherry Creek Presbyterian Church (EPC) in Greenwood Village, Colorado.

George went to Moody Bible Institute (diploma), and received his BA from Gordon College. He has also received numerous honorary doctorates.

Don also holds a degree from Moody Bible Institute (diploma). He went on to Lawrence University in Appleton, Wisconsin (BA), Oxford University in England (MA), and Trinity Evangelical Divinity School, in Deerfield, Illinois (PhD, in church history).

George served as the sixth president of Moody Bible Institute, and more recently in the roles of chancellor and chancellor emeritus.

Don was recently inaugurated as the president of Reformed Theological Seminary in Orlando, Florida.

Both of us have been pastors and presidents of theological institutions training leaders. One of us is an evangelist by gifting. The other is a pastor-teacher. One is Baptist. The other is Presbyterian. One is more reformed, and the other is less so.

Yet, out of an experience of two lives (one eight decades long, another five decades long), as a father-son team who love and respect each other, we each offer useful insights about how to approach life's finish line. We write from a pastor's perspective.

So this book is a collaboration. It draws heavily on the words and experiences of George Sweeting but also includes insights from Don. In some ways it is like Johnny Cash's final recordings. You hear the gravelly voice of an older man, produced with the help of a younger musician to enhance the tunes nevertheless. Both of us fit Puritan Richard Baxter's description, who said, "I preach as never sure to preach again, as a dying man to dying men."[3]

THE BOOK AT A GLANCE

Let me give you a thumbnail sketch of this book.

The first chapter focuses on how we should think about our entire spiritual journey—is it a marathon or a sprint? The second chapter deals with how to stay young on the inside while our bodies rebel. It looks at the relevance of the gospel in the second half of life. The third chapter looks back on life lessons: "Wisdom Insights of an Octogenarian." Chapter 4 focuses on retirement. How should we think about it? Is the retirement dream a Western construct or a biblical concept?

Chapter 5 covers the importance of not giving up on younger people, but investing in them. Chapter 6 talks about transitions and how to navigate them. Chapter 7 looks at some pacesetters, people in our lives who have gone the distance—they have run the race and give us examples to follow. Chapter 8 covers how we should think about and what we should do with our possessions.

Chapter 9 examines the reality, the inevitability, and the meaning of suffering. Chapter 10 looks at the "bucket list" and sets forth one incredibly important way to revise it. Chapter 11 is titled "The Best Funerals I Ever Attended." Without being morbid, it considers how to plan for our own service. Chapter 12 is on some of the habits of those who finish well, and some of the temptations that cause second-halfers to crash.

Chapter 13, "The Somber Season," addresses the challenge of terminal illness and slow death. Chapter 14 covers what the Puritans called "dying well." The final chapter focuses on the realities of heaven and hell.

All of these are important subjects for anyone in the second half of life. But here's the rub. Most people in our culture do not plan carefully for this season. If they do any planning at all, it's usually confined to finances. Yet life, and certainly the Christian life, involves so much more.

As you can see, this book is filled with both realism and hope. We believe it will help you think straight about your final years, whenever they might come. Underneath everything we write lies a conviction we share with the apostle Paul, who told a group of Christ followers in Philippi, "I am sure of this, that he who began a good work in you will bring it to completion at the day of Jesus Christ" (Philippians 1:6 ESV).

So take a moment right now, before you go any further, and offer a quick prayer. Ask God to teach you through these pages. Thank Him for the good work He has begun in your life. Pray that He gives you the grace to finish with strength.

1

LONG-DISTANCE CHRISTIANITY

"EIGHTY YEARS HAVE I SERVED HIM."
—POLYCARP, BISHOP OF SMYRNA, AD 155

RECENTLY WHILE SITTING on an airplane, someone asked me what metaphors I use to describe my life. It's not every day you get that question. But it is a lot more interesting question than being asked, "How's the weather?" "What do you do?" or, "How about them Broncos?"

CHOOSE YOUR METAPHOR

People use different metaphors to describe their lives. Remember *Forrest Gump*? "Life is like a box of chocolates. You never know what you're going to get."

For others, life is a song—a creative expression. From birth to death, you are working on your own signature composition. Remember *Mr. Holland's Opus*?

For still others, life is a game, or life is a dream, or a battle, or a roller coaster. I have a friend who truly believes life is a party; the point of being alive is to just have fun.

To be honest, no one metaphor captures our entire lives. But for both of us, the journey metaphor describes our lives more than any other. Life is a long journey.

Both of us have been captured by that great Christian classic *Pilgrim's Progress*, which also highlights this theme. John Bunyan wrote the book while in prison in the late 1600s. The original title was really long but highlights the basic idea: *The Pilgrim's Progress From This World to That Which is to Come: Delivered under the similitude of a dream wherein is discovered the manner of his setting out, his dangerous journey; and safe arrival at the desired country.*

Granted, you'll never see a title that long today. Bunyan presents the Christian life as a journey with a start and a finish. It takes us from the city of man (the City of Destruction) to the city of God (the celestial or heavenly city). In that journey, progress is important. You are never safe until you are home. Detours abound. And finishing well is vital.

One reason this metaphor appeals to us is because the Bible repeatedly uses journey language.

JOURNEY LANGUAGE IN THE BIBLE

Think of Adam and Eve leaving Eden. Or Abraham leaving Ur. Think of Israel leaving Egypt on their way to the Promised Land. Think of the Jewish people's journey into exile and the return under Ezra.

In the New Testament, several writers speak of the Christian life as a special kind of journey—a race. In Philippians 3:13–14, Paul writes, "Forgetting what is behind and straining toward what is ahead, I press on toward the goal to win the prize for which God has called me heavenward in Christ Jesus." In 2 Timothy 4:7, writing of the end of his life, he says, "I have finished the race."

The writer of Hebrews says, "Let us run with perseverance the race marked out for us" (Hebrews 12:1). He is thinking of a certain kind of race—not a sprint but a distance event.

The Christian life is not a hundred-yard dash . . . but more like a marathon!

Recently one member of our family ran in the Chicago Marathon. A marathon is a long race—26.2 miles. You have to be in real good shape to enter. Participants have six and a half hours in which to finish the course. The winning time in that race was 2:06:24.

I heard someone say the first part of a marathon is like a party. There are all these runners—in Chicago there were forty-five thousand. Crowds lined the streets. The runners started in Grant Park by Lake Michigan. They ran through ethnic neighborhoods from the North Side to the South Side. But after about ten miles, the party was definitely over. That's when runners begin to look pale. At mile thirteen you "hit the wall." Some exhausted runners start collapsing. You can see them lying on cots on the side of the road. A marathon is a serious, long-distance run.

Being a disciple of Jesus is like that. We're called not to a quick sprint but to a long, arduous journey!

During the 1968 Olympics in Mexico City, runner John Stephen Akhwari of Tanzania competed with seventy-four other world-class runners. Akhwari did not win the race. Actually, he came in last! But he is remembered for *how* he ran the race.

Halfway through the marathon, Akhwari fell and badly injured his leg, dislocating a joint. After a few minutes on the ground, John Akhwari did what most runners would never do.

He picked himself up off the ground, strapped up his leg, and continued to run.

About an hour after the winner had crossed the finish line, and with only a few thousand spectators left in the stadium, word got out about what had happened to Akhwari. He was still running. When he finally entered the stadium, his leg was bloody and bandaged. Every step caused him to wince. But the remaining crowd began to clap. He turned the curve, and the crowd grew louder. As he approached the finish line and hobbled across, they cheered wildly as if he had won the race. They were stunned by his endurance.

Afterward, when the press asked him why he ran through the pain, despite the fact he could not win, Akhwari looked perplexed. "I don't think you understand," he said. "My country did not send me seven thousand miles to start the race. They sent me seven thousand miles to *finish the race*."[1]

This is a great image of endurance for us to keep in mind as we consider long-distance Christianity. The Christian life is, as Eugene Peterson described it in his book on the Psalms, "a long obedience in the same direction." It's a marathon. It requires commitment and discipline to the very end.

Scripture often speaks of the importance of "continuing." In my old King James Bible, it says of the early disciples that in the upper room, they "all continued with one accord in prayer" (Acts 1:14 NKJV). It also says "they continued steadfastly in the apostles' doctrine and fellowship" (Acts 2:42 NKJV). This language runs through the New Testament. They continued in faith and in love.

In Philippians 1:25, Paul says, "I will continue with all of you for your progress and joy in the faith." Colossians 2:6 says, "As you received Christ Jesus as Lord, continue to live in him."

LIVING IN A CULTURE OF QUITTING

Recently I've heard a news commentator say that we live in a culture of quitting. This individual was complaining about the high turnover of computer technicians in the workplace. People tend not to stick around one place too long. One of my children started a job after high school. After several weeks, he wanted to quit because it was hard. I would not allow it!

Think of all the people who start—but soon quit—diets and fitness routines. Think of the many who start attending church, only to leave after a short while. Worse yet, think of all those who start a marriage but then leave when things become difficult.

Colleges constantly deal with retention issues. Many students who start, drop out.

High school graduation rates in America are also trending downward. Rates peaked in 1969, at 77 percent, but are now at 68 percent. This means 32 percent of high school students do not finish. A recent report said that seventeen of the nation's fifty largest cities had high school graduation rates lower than 50 percent![2]

It is easy to quit when things get difficult. The Christian's journey is filled with many hard things. Trials will come. Doubts will arise. Disappointments come unexpectedly. People you trust will let you down. Church conflict may disillusion you. You will fail

more than you ever thought possible. You will most likely be in-
sulted for your faith. Perhaps you will be persecuted. No doubt you
will grow weary from this long journey.

In Hebrews 12, after exhorting us to "run with perseverance
the race marked out for us," the writer tells us to look to Jesus, "the
author and perfecter of our faith." Verse 3 says, "Consider him who
endured such opposition from sinful men, so that you will not grow
weary and lose heart."

Like an athlete running a long-distance race, whose legs want
to stop, whose lungs are not getting enough oxygen, and who is
growing weary and ready to bonk, the journeying Christian will
grow weary of doing good (Galatians 6) and will want to give up.
We will have good days, but we will also have plenty of bad days.
We will be tempted to want to take shortcuts or drop out of the
race altogether.

At that very moment we have two encouragements to keep us
going. There is the "great cloud of witnesses," whose example, like
the stadium spectators of old, cheer us on to stay in the race. But
more importantly, we have the Lord Himself going ahead of us,
"who for the joy set before him endured the cross, scorning its
shame, and sat down at the right hand of the throne of God" (Hebrews 12:2). His encouragement is there so we will not grow weary
and lose heart.

He not only gives us the grace and grit to carry on when we
feel like quitting, but He also holds out for us the ultimate future
and eternal joy we will share with Him at the end of our race. This
is what enables His saints to persevere in the Christian marathon.
This is what enables us to keep going.

AN EXAMPLE FROM THE EARLY CHURCH

One of the great examples of enduring faithfulness in the early church was a man named Polycarp of Smyrna. A prominent city pastor of a church in Asia Minor (now Turkey), he was martyred in AD 155.

Polycarp was born about AD 69, around the time of Paul's martyrdom in Rome. His church may actually have been established by Paul. Polycarp was even discipled by the apostle John! Early church leader Irenaeus says that Polycarp had talked to many who had seen Christ.

We have a detailed account of Polycarp's death in the writings of Eusebius, the early church historian. He was executed under the reign of the Roman emperor Antoninus Pius during a wave of persecution.

When Christians were being fed to wild beasts in the arena, a crowd began to chant, "Away with the atheists! Find Polycarp!" (Pagans sometimes called Christians atheists because Christians refused to believe in the gods.)

At this time, Polycarp was an old man. When the authorities searched for and found the elderly pastor, they arrested him and brought him to the arena. First they tried to persuade him to curse Christ and confess Caesar as Lord in order to save himself.

At the judgment seat, the governor said, "Curse Christ and I will release you. Have respect for your old age. Say, 'Away with the atheists!'"

The old bishop replied, "Eighty-six years I have served Christ and He has done me no wrong. How then can I blaspheme my King who has saved me?"[3]

That's long-distance Christianity!

They threatened Polycarp with wild beasts, but he would not be dissuaded. The proconsul then threatened to burn him alive.

Polycarp replied, "You threaten fire that burns for an hour and is over. But the judgment on the ungodly is forever."

The fire was then prepared. Polycarp lifted his eyes to heaven and prayed: "Father, I bless You that You deemed me worthy of this day and hour, that I might take a portion of the martyrs in the cup of Christ... Among these may I today be welcome before Thy face as a rich and acceptable sacrifice."

The flames then engulfed him, and he was burned alive!

Not all those who confessed Christ as Savior in the early church were that steadfast. Some gave in to the pressure to preserve their lives. Some burned incense to Caesar, cursed Christ, and fell away. Rather than finish the race, they quit when it got hard. That's always the way it has been.

BILLY AND CHUCK

Back in 1944, as a student at Moody Bible Institute, I (George) remember listening to some influential preachers who were involved with a new organization called Youth for Christ. Two of them stood out—young Billy Graham and young Chuck Templeton. Of the two, it seemed that Templeton was the more gifted. Some called him the most brilliant, dynamic young preacher in America. He and Billy were close friends. I heard Chuck preach at Moody Church. He not only preached, but he also drew an illustrative chalk drawing as he preached, as I later did.

Templeton pastored a church in Toronto. He then went to

Princeton and became an evangelist of the Presbyterian Church USA. After Princeton, Templeton broadened his message. By 1950 he had left the ministry to pursue a radio and television career. Eventually he said he no longer believed that Jesus was the Son of God, and he became an atheist. Chuck Templeton did not continue.

Billy, of course, followed a different path. It's not that he didn't face temptation and doubt. Read his biography. It is clear that he did. But he continued in the faith. Well into his 90s, he still proclaims Christ and His gospel.

Maybe you know people like Templeton—people who at one point appeared to be on fire for God but have since dropped out. And maybe you know others who are still persevering, living out a long-distance faith.

What causes one person to stay on course, and another to fall away? I know that Billy Graham and others like him would answer that their endurance is ultimately by God's grace.

HOW DO WE REMAIN STEADFAST? A PRELIMINARY RESPONSE

But humanly speaking, what explains the difference? And how do we remain steadfast and stick with the race? This whole book seeks to answer these questions. But here is an initial response.

First, those who practice long-distance Christianity have a marathon mind-set. They consider the long view and know that this is a lifelong journey with many seasons. In this race they understand that God is faithful. But like an athlete, they also understand the importance of constancy of purpose. So they run with the end in view. They keep their eyes fixed on the finish line and the prize. They know they must "lay aside every weight," including the sins that slow us down, so that they can make it to the end (Hebrews 12:1 ESV). Perhaps that's why the New Testament repeatedly uses athletic illustrations to describe the life of the Christian. Something like athletic discipline is necessary to reach the finish line of faith.

Second, we remain steadfast by taking advantage of all the encouragements and means of persevering grace that God gives His people to stay on track. We have God's Word, the Bible, to help us renew our minds and cleanse our hearts. We have the gift of the church. The worship and fellowship of the church are absolutely necessary for us to stay faithful.

Solo Christianity does not work. The fire of our own faith is enhanced as we stay near the fire of other people's faith. Isolate an ember and it quickly dies out. Gather them together and the fire stays hot. In the fellowship of the local church, we have regular corporate worship and fellowship to restore our spiritual bearings. The preached Word is one of the main ways God speaks to us. Communion and baptism are gospel signs to remind us who we are in Christ and the strength of His love for us. They are occasions to renew our covenant commitment to the Lord.

Third, we have the help of the Lord Himself, by the Holy Spirit, who said He would never leave us or forsake us. He promises to be with us to the end of our lives. As we trust Him, He gives us strength to continue. As we grow more deeply in His gospel, He confirms and affirms our faith.

Neither of us authors knows how many years we have left. We are both in the second half of life. We may be near the end of life, or quite far from the end. George has had cancer twice—once as a teen, and once in his 60s. He never expected to live this long. So he has been thinking about this topic for a long time. Don also has had some close calls. Statistically, someone in their 80s has a shorter time left than someone in their fifties. Statistically, fifty-year-olds have twenty-five or more years left. But neither of us has a clue how many days God has ordained for us.

We share a sense that today is a day of grace—that each day is a gift, and that we want to make each one count until we reach that finish line.

A number of years ago, I (Don) observed a baptism service in England at an Anglican church. New believers were being baptized. After baptizing each individual, the minister signed each person with the sign of the cross and said, "I sign you with the cross, the sign of Christ. Do not be ashamed to confess your faith in Christ crucified. Fight valiantly under the banner of Christ against sin, the world, and the Devil, *and continue* as His faithful soldier and servant to the end of your life."

Continue! Continue! We leave that charge with you as you think about a long-distance faith.

2

THE GOSPEL FOR THE SECOND HALF

Staying Young Inside as Your Body Ages

"WE HAVE THIS TREASURE IN JARS OF CLAY."
—2 CORINTHIANS 4:7

IT IS CURIOUS to watch the baby boom generation age. This massive generation, part of which is now entering retirement, attempts to transform whatever it touches. They've left their imprint on each phase of life through which they've passed. They've transformed music and pop culture. They've delayed marriage, have divorced more often, and have had fewer kids. They've transformed approaches to parenting. They've changed the way we think about jobs with multiple careers and reinventions. They opened the doors to adult learning. And now they are trying to redefine retirement and aging!

OUR BLISSFUL DENIAL

Baby boomers bring to retirement a vision of ageless old age where the 60s are the new 40s, the 70s are the new 50s, and the 80s are the new 60s. They have no interest in giving up what they believe is rightly theirs—perpetual youth. With enough supplements, surgeries, and botox, they hope to defy old age.

But boomers, like every other generation, are in for a reality check. All the resveratrol, green tea, wrinkle creams, garlic, and wishful thinking in the world will not prevent the onset of old age. Despite extended life spans, the fact of growing older and the challenge of aging bodies are not a respecter of demographic prowess. Sooner or later, everyone has to face up to their own mortality.

Consider what happens to you after age 30. Your bones have stopped growing and start becoming thinner and weaker as you move into midlife. We hit maximum muscle mass at age 30; after that, muscles begin to reduce in size. Along with that, your joints become less flexible, and vertebral discs may begin to deteriorate.

Between ages 30 and 70, your brain will decrease about 10 percent in size as it loses neurons and memory grows less sharp.[1] In your 40s and 50s, your heart becomes less efficient, blood vessels lose elasticity, and fatty deposits may begin to clog your arteries. Besides that, your arteries are less flexible and your blood pressure starts to go up.

In that same time, the volume of your lungs decreases and becomes less efficient. After 30 your intestines slow down, along with your metabolism. The more it slows, the easier it is to gain weight. In your 40s, as they say, "shift happens," and that weight starts to settle in new places. Your kidneys lose efficiency. Your retinas will thin, and lenses will get cloudy. Your hearing will grow weaker. It's payback for all that loud music you listened to as a teen.

In your 50s your legs will probably start to resemble road maps. Some of us will start to develop what they call "turkey neck." And if that doesn't happen, your chin will have twins. This is also the era when those early fillings fall out of your teeth and you begin to talk about crowns and root canals.

Besides changing color, your hair gets thinner, if it does not disappear altogether. Some time after your hair disappears, it's the revenge of all those bad childhood sunburns. Wrinkles and blotches appear! It's amazing how that happens. And this is just a partial list. Need I say more? The truth of the matter is, in the second half of life we are all wearing out.

And the bad news is not just for the over-thirty crowd! Whether you are young, old, or. . . . "mature and holding," all of us have to reckon with the effects of aging. We begin to notice the deterioration in late childhood. That's when we start getting fillings and wearing glasses. That's when, from all our sports dedication, ankles begin to sprain, hamstrings rupture, knees get blown, groins get pulled, tears show up in the Achilles tendon, and carpal tunnel syndrome develops. The wear from sports and exercise comes back to haunt us in the form of "overuse" injuries.

All this bad body news should puncture the baby boomer balloon. Yet we keep telling ourselves we will be the first to defy the drag of aging. Despite the mounting evidence, many continue in a state of blissful denial.

SLOWING IT DOWN

This is not to ignore all those strategies you hear about slowing the aging process. By taking care of ourselves, we can slow the clock. True chronological age does not necessarily correlate with functional age.

There's lots of stuff written now about how to be 100. It will help if we:

1. Exercise regularly—both aerobically and with weights. If nothing else, walk or swim.
2. Don't smoke and avoid substance abuse of all kinds.
3. Get regular physicals, blood tests (men, prostate; women, breast), and dental checkups.
4. Watch what you eat, limit dietary fats, take in fewer calories, and eat fewer processed or refined foods. Instead, consume plenty of fruits and vegetables.
5. Wear your seat belts or helmets when you ride.
6. Keep your mind active, and don't stop learning. It is good for the brain.
7. Avoid social isolation. Have a best friend or a pet, and do things with people. This also extends life.
8. Avoid too much sun and use sunscreen with good UV protection.
9. Get enough sleep.
10. Have faith—people of faith live longer. Many studies now show that being part of a church or a community of faith actually extends life.

I (George) write about some of these subjects at greater length in my book on successful aging, where I urge us all to be "temple keepers." Our bodies are the temple of God, and we have a responsibility to be good stewards of what God's given to us. I believe in doing these things (though I am better at some than others). This has enabled me to live into my upper 80s, to enjoy my children, my grandchildren, and even my great-grandchildren. It has allowed me to bless my wife for over sixty years, and to serve in ministry for almost seventy years. Humanly speaking, taking care of yourself can extend your life impact.

But having said all that, and having written a book entitled *The Joys of Successful Aging*, there comes a day when the "successful" part is not there as much as it used to be!

It is a biblical truth that "our outer nature is wasting away." Don was recently complaining about a knee injury. I told him to quit whining. "Son, when you get to my age, it's not just your knee that hurts. Everything hurts! I have a long list of things I could tell you that hurt. In fact, at my age, if it ain't hurtin', it probably ain't workin'!" The older you get, the more your body groans with the rest of creation!

A TREASURE IN CLAY JARS

But the other part of 2 Corinthians 4:16 states that while this is happening, "inwardly we are being renewed day by day." That's what caused Paul not to lose heart. In other words, there is a way to stay young inside while your body ages.

Earlier in his second letter to the Corinthians, the apostle wrote, "But we have this treasure in jars of clay" (2 Corinthians 4:7). What does he mean?

Paul encountered the glory of God in the face of Christ when he met Jesus on the Damascus road. Since that time he began to proclaim the glorious light of the gospel. So in this text, he compares the gospel to a treasure, and his aging body to a clay jar that holds it. Let's think for a moment about these powerful but contrasting images.

"Jars of clay" back then was not a music group, but were earthen pots. Unlike the more expensive bronze pots, they were cheap, easily broken, and readily discarded. Such containers would often hold food, water, or wine—but not a rich treasure.

When you think of a great treasure, what comes to mind? Perhaps you picture the famed Fabergé eggs or maybe the British crown jewels. Then again, these days maybe you imagine a gold bar weighing 100 ounces. That's what we think treasure looks like.

But Paul begs to differ. He has something far more valuable in mind. Here the treasure is the gospel, or as verse 6 puts it, "the light of the knowledge of the glory of God in the face of Christ" (ESV).

In the Bible, the gospel is compared to a priceless treasure. It is the pearl of great price (Matthew 13:45–46). It is worth far more than any other treasure you can imagine because it involves the riches of God in Jesus—and the unsurpassed glory of Christ. This is His precious grace gift that comes to us through the cross and resurrection.

You would expect the world's greatest treasure to be held in a vault, not a clay pot. But this treasure, when entrusted to people like us, is contained in earthen vessels.

WHAT IS THE GOSPEL THAT WE HOLD?

Let's be clear about what we mean by the gospel. The gospel is the best news on earth. It is the message about God's saving grace in Jesus Christ to a lost humanity. It tells us how God rescues us from sin, death, and hell. It is good news from God (Romans 1:1). It is about a plan conceived by the Trinity in eternity past that brought to fulfillment His ancient promise to bless the nations of the earth.

This gospel is centered in the person and achievement of Jesus—His incarnation as the infinite, eternal God man, His righteousness as the new Adam, His atoning death as the Lamb who takes away the sin of the world, and His bodily resurrection as the firstborn of the new creation. The gospel concerns what was achieved by that great saving act—that righteousness was fulfilled, sin was paid for, and the perfect guilt offering satisfied the rigteous demands of God's justice. Because of all this, death fell apart and the grave could not hold Jesus.

The gospel is about how by grace through faith you and I can be pardoned of all our sins and accepted by Him—that is justified! It is about how we can be declared "not guilty" of our sins and then adopted into God's family. It is about how we can be delivered from the power of evil through Christ who is stronger.

But that is not all. The gospel is also about Christ's exaltation as Lord to the right hand of the Father, where He was given a place of universal authority. It is about the victory and presence of His kingdom. It is about His return as judge of all the earth when He will visibly bring all things under His rule in a new heaven and earth.

Yet there is more. It is about how He saved me for Himself, that I might be reconciled to heaven so I can know God, enjoy Him, serve Him, and find my true satisfaction in Him.

This gospel is the most important news in the world. It is what the world needs more than anything else. It is as simple as John

3:16, as deep as the book of Romans, and as broad as the story of the whole Bible.

When each of us first heard the gospel, perhaps as children from our parents, we knew it was good news, but we had no idea how profoundly earthshaking it really was.

In different circumstances, we simply recognized it as the simple truth that Jesus is life! Christ died for our sins and saved us from eternal death so we could live a new kind of life. Early on it was not much more complicated than "Jesus loves me, this I know, for the Bible tells me so." But back then, we did not imagine how great a salvation it was. The truth is, we still can't fathom the "depth of the riches of the wisdom and knowledge of God" (Romans 11:33). Through our lives, each of us keeps coming to new points on the journey where we discover something more about God's deep and amazing love for us in Christ. And until the end of our lives, and even through eternity, there will be more to discover.

It is this gospel that has been entrusted to us (Galatians 2:7). We hold it in the clay pots of the bodies that we've been given.

So here we all are, in the second half of life, and we find that the gospel, this treasure, is inexhaustible because God is inexhaustible.

Why is it, we wonder, that people think of the gospel as something for new believers only? Why is it that so many of us live as if the gospel is just about how to begin the Christian life—and not relevant to the middle and also the end of the Christian life? And why are we so slow to realize this? We've finally come to that place where we believe the gospel is as relevant to the second half of life as it is to the first half!

GOOD NEWS FOR SECOND-HALFERS

You ask, how? Let us name just a few areas. Consider the matter of our identity. When we are justified by grace, we gain a new identity. We are now "in Christ." Our sins are pardoned. We are reconciled to and accepted by our heavenly Father through Christ. He gives us a new identity card.

That's pretty relevant for people in a rapidly changing job market, where layoffs come faster than we expect and suddenly our career is over and our professional identity is challenged. That's when men and women often wonder who they are. They think, I was an engineer, I was a teacher, I was a CFO—but now that I've lost my job, who am I? If your identity is based on your profession and not your relationship with God, then you are in for a shock. But if you have put your trust in Jesus as Savior and Lord, your primary identity remains in Christ. Your significance transcends your career. You are still called to serve and enjoy Him, and still loved deeply by your heavenly Father.

Or consider the topic of forgiveness. We have seen too many friends come to the end of their lives and become overwhelmed by all of the wrong they did in their past. The Devil will often dredge up all the sins of your past and accuse you. But the gospel reminds us that God's love for us rests not on our performance but on Christ's. He has more grace for us than we have mistakes. In one of the most wonderful verses in the Bible, God declares, "There is therefore now no condemnation for those who are in Christ Jesus" (Romans 8:1 ESV). The matter of our forgiveness is settled.

How about the issue of eternal life? As you get closer to the end of your life, the big questions start popping up: Where, when, and how will I die? What happens after I die? As you get older, you sometimes have more time to ponder such things. Or you don't sleep as well at night, so you wake up and think about things. Like, Where will my soul be the moment my brain waves stop and my heartbeat falls off? But if you are grounded in the gospel, you know that nothing can separate you from His love (Romans 8).

What about the issue of rest? One of the authors of this book is a bit weary. The other is living pretty fast. The one who is tired is running out of energy. When you are in your 80s, rest is more important than ever. So the thought of Jesus saying, "Come to me, all you who are weary and burdened, and I will give you rest," (Matthew 11:28) sounds pretty good. When the writer of Hebrews says, "There remains, then, a Sabbath-rest for the people of God; for anyone who enters God's rest also rests from his own work, just as God did from his" (4:9–10), heavenly rests sounds like relief— like sliding into bed at the end of the day when you're dead tired. There is nothing like it.

Or how about the thought of a resurrection body? That part of the gospel sounds real promising.

What about freedom from oppression and the hope of entering our Promised Land? Millions long for this.

Each of these applications of the gospel has real attraction in the second half of life. They fill us with hope. So that, in spite of the fact that our pots crack and our knees creak, we find ourselves renewed on the inside—staying young while our bodies rebel. Why? Because we hold this treasure on the inside.

Let's end this chapter with a few quick applications. If the gospel we hold is this important, what should we do with it for our remaining days on the journey? Let us suggest three things.

First, pass on the gospel. Live and speak the good news. Or as Mark 16:15 puts it, "Go into all the world and preach the gospel to all creation." Why? Because it is our only hope. There is so much hopelessness in our society. In contrast, people of hope stand out. As the Holy Spirit prompts you, "be prepared to . . . give the reason for the hope that you have " (1 Peter 3:15).

Share the treasure. As you do, make sure people know that you are not pointing to yourself but to Christ in you, the hope of glory. We are way too timid about this. We don't have to be obnoxious about it. But we have to get the word out. Telling about the treasure is one of the greatest acts of love you could ever do for another person. Lovingly, creatively, prayerfully, winsomely, but definitely, share the gospel with others.

Second, explore and revel in the gospel. I think you now realize this treasure is worth far more than you suspected. Stop underestimating the gospel and get to know it. See how its message really is the big story of the whole Bible. See how it unfolds in God's revelation. As you read God's Word, you will see that the gospel is like a diamond. Examine it and you will see its brilliance every time you turn it over in your mind. Its beauty will cause you to grow in gratitude as you praise God for it.

Third, preach the gospel to yourself. The gospel is not just for non-Christians. It is for you. Daily believe it. Daily embrace Christ. Some of the early church fathers thought of the gospel as medicine for every day. Now that's a relevant image for some of us! Take it in daily, then watch how God transforms your inner nature.

It's been said that when you are young, the past looks short, and the future looks long. But when you are old, the past looks long, and the future looks short. At late middle age, most people reach a tipping point and tend to look backward and dwell on the past.

But the gospel changes all that. It blows open the future and makes it look long again. It causes us to stay young on the inside, even while our body ages.

3

WISDOM INSIGHTS OF AN OCTOGENARIAN

"TEACH US TO NUMBER OUR DAYS ARIGHT,
THAT WE MAY GAIN A HEART OF WISDOM."
—Psalm 90:12

A LAWYER AND a senior citizen are sitting next to each other on a long flight. The lawyer is thinking that seniors are so dumb; he could get one over on this guy easily. So the lawyer asks if the senior would like to play a game. The senior just wants to take a nap, so he politely declines and tries to catch a few winks.

The lawyer persists, saying the game is a lot of fun. "I ask you a question, and if you don't know the answer, you pay me only five dollars. Then you ask me one, and if I don't know the answer, I will pay you five hundred dollars."

This catches the senior's attention. To keep the lawyer quiet, he agrees to play the game.

The lawyer asks the first question. "What's the distance from the Earth to the moon?"

The senior doesn't say a word, but reaches into his pocket, pulls out a five dollar bill, and hands it to the lawyer.

Now, it's the senior's turn. He asks the lawyer, "What goes up a hill with three legs and comes down with four?"

The lawyer uses his laptop to search all the references he can find on the Internet.

He sends emails to all his brilliant lawyer friends, but none can give him the answer. After thirty minutes of searching, he finally says, "I give up." He wakes the senior and hands him a check for five hundred dollars. The senior pockets the check and goes back to sleep.

Meanwhile, not knowing the answer is driving the lawyer crazy. So he wakes the old man and asks, "So what goes up a hill with three legs and comes down with four?"

The senior reaches into his pocket, hands the lawyer five dollars, and goes back to sleep!

Beware of underestimating the wisdom of seniors!

AGE AND WISDOM

In our culture, the only equation we make between age and wisdom is that young people are wise, while old people are hopelessly out-of-date and irrelevant. But according to the Bible, we have it backward. In Scripture, the young person gets wisdom from the older person; that is the consistent pattern.

There is a whole body of wisdom literature in the Bible that throws a wet blanket on the conventional thinking of our culture. In one wisdom book, Job says, "Is not wisdom found among the aged? Does not long life bring understanding?" (Job 12:12). In another wisdom book, Proverbs, the aged are perceived as resourceful people who are encouraged to train younger people in wisdom.

And the young are admonished to listen to their words and learn the lessons of life. "Listen, my son, to your father's instruction and do not forsake your mother's teaching. They will be a garland to grace your head and a chain to adorn your neck" (Proverbs 1:8–9).

We've titled this chapter "Wisdom Insights of an Octogenarian." Are you familiar with that word? Age can be divided in different ways. Some do it this way. There's infancy, childhood, preadolescence, adolescence, early adulthood (20–39), middle adulthood (40–59), and late adulthood (60+). Late adulthood can be divided as well. Some speak of the young old (65–74), the middle old (75–84), and the oldest old (85+).

But age can also be divided by decade. If you are in your 50s, you are a quinquagenarian; if you are in your 60s, you are a sexagenarian; if you are in your 70s, you are a septuagenarian; if you are in your 80s, you are an octogenarian. If you make it to the 90s, you will be a nonagenarian. If you hit 100, you will be a centenarian. Those 110 and older are called supercentenarians!

I, George, write as an octogenarian. And in this chapter I want to share some wisdom lessons from living eight decades.

Moses had people like me in mind when he wrote Psalm 90. He said, "The length of our days is seventy years—or eighty, if we have the strength" (v. 10).

This is a great psalm. It reminds us that God Himself, the everlasting One, is our home. Verse 1 reads, "Lord, you have been our dwelling place throughout all generations . . . from everlasting to everlasting you are God" (vv. 1–2).

People, on the other hand, are compared to dust or grass (vv. 3–6). We rise up in the morning like new grass. But by evening we are already withered.

Not only are we frail, but we are also under God's holy wrath. How often we forget this! We live our lives under the curse of Adam. So it can rightly be said that "all our days pass away under your wrath" (v. 9).

Given our finiteness and sin, and God's infiniteness and holiness, the psalmist prays, "Teach us to number our days aright, that we may gain a heart of wisdom" (90:12).

When you live to be 80, you learn a thing or two. You've seen a lot of life. Here are a few of the lessons I've learned through eight decades. So let me, for a moment, play the role of the sage in Proverbs, while you take the role of the student. As Solomon wrote to his son, let me echo his words to you: "Make your ear attentive to wisdom, incline your heart to understanding" (Proverbs 2:2 NASB).

SOME LESSONS FROM AN OCTOGENARIAN

First, life is short.

I was born in 1924. As a child in the 1930s, I remember that life seemed to move very slowly. I remember thinking that my summer vacation from school seemed like it would never end. Time crawled from day to day. So much so, that by August I could hardly wait to get back to school.

Each day I had chores. It was my job to beat and clean the throw rugs from our floors. Then I'd have to weed the garden. After that work was done, my mother would say that I was free to play. The rest of my days alternated between wading in the brook behind my house, catching crayfish, watching birds, picking berries, playing marathon Monopoly . . . or baseball. Sometimes we would even skinny-dip! We called our little brook BAB, which to my parents meant "Best American Beach," but to us it meant something else . . . because we were naked! Mother would say, "Where are you going?" and we would say, "Out." Then she would ask, "What are you going to do?" And we'd answer, "Nothing!"

The tempo of life picked up in my teen years. My first outside job came when I was 11. It was picking beans at a local farm from 8:00 a.m. to 5:00 p.m. I hated it . . . and knew right then that the Lord did not want me to become a farmer.

The following year I worked on a milk truck delivering milk for the Franklin Lakes Dairy from midnight to 8:00 a.m. for a dollar a day. I did that until age 17. I also drove the truck, before it was even legal for me to drive. My parents didn't know that either! To get up at midnight meant I had to go to bed by 7:00 p.m.

All this took place during the Great Depression. I had all the milk I wanted to drink, for free!

But when I was paid, 10 percent of my pay was for my tithe to our church, 10 percent went into my savings account, 10 percent was for me to spend, if necessary, and 70 percent went my parents, to help pay for our house mortgage.

From college on, my pace of life accelerated. It started to dawn on me that life is very short and fragile. Now, at age 87, I see what the Bible means when it says that life is like the weaver's shuttle or like a vapor that appears for a moment.

The older I get, the faster it seems to go. I've often said that life is so short, the wood of our cradle rubs up against the wood of our casket.

When I talk to young people, I sometimes say, "Whatever you are going to do, do it now." You have a little window of maybe thirty to forty years to make any significant contribution, if you are blessed with good health. Get on with it!

Second, life has its seasons.

For that matter, almost everything has its season. Nature has winter, spring, summer, and fall. Each sport has its season. Even products have life cycles. In Ecclesiastes 3:1 we read, "There is a time for everything, and a season for every activity under heaven." Life happens in seasons. I believe God designed it this way.

Each season has its own character, with its own blessings and challenges. Some seasons are stormier than others. Some are prettier. But they do not last. The cycle is always moving.

Fruit comes in season. It doesn't come right away. Don just planted a lemon tree in his backyard. But the horticulturalist told him it would be three years before he would really see fruit come from it. Though he wants it right away, he must wait.

The important thing is to know which season you are in—and make the most of it. When you make a decision, think about its impact three to five years off in the next season.

Retired auto executive Lee Iacocca wrote that there are three phases of life: "learn, earn, and return." He said the first third of your life is the "learn" phase. Much of it is devoted to education. The second phase is the "earn" phase; you build a career and make a living. Then comes the final third, devoted to giving back and returning in gratitude.[1]

I understand where Iacocca is coming from, but the problem with putting it this way is that it is very unwise to ever stop learning. Furthermore, given the economy, it will take more than the second third of your life to make a living. And if you think gratitude should be confined to the last part of life, you are crazy!

I think it is more helpful to think of life like nature's seasons. As Ecclesiastes says, "There is . . . a time to be born." That's life's springtime—a phase in which we need nurture and teaching. Parents play a key role and help us develop basic character and skills. Then other teachers enter our lives and build on that foundation.

Next comes "a time to plant" (early summer). In this phase of life, we use what we have learned. We hear God's call, make sense of it, and finish our basic training. We graduate and launch out into our first assignment. We begin to use our talents and develop patterns. It's also a season to raise families.

Then comes late summer when our firstfruits begins to be harvested. We see who we are becoming, and our life themes emerge.

This is followed by early fall, "a time to reap." I love the fall with its harvests. To me it symbolizes a full and satisfying life. In this season, we see the results of all the seeds we've planted. Our fruits show themselves.

Then comes late fall. Depending on where you live, this can be a season of magnificent color.

This is followed by life's winter, "a time to die." Though the Bible says we can still bear fruit, even into old age, our energies begin to noticeably subside. Winter is a season full of all kinds of transitions.

What season are you in? Are you making the most of it and awake to its unique possibilities and challenges?

Third, God is sovereign over all life.

This biblical truth becomes more important to me the older I get. I find great comfort in the words of that simple chorus, "He's got the whole world in His hands." He's got me, and my loved ones, and the whole world.

Biblically speaking, the good news about life's passages is that God's mercies are new, not just every morning but also every season. He stands sovereignly over them. When at last life's winter comes, there is yet, in Christ, the promise of something more—another springtime!

I (George) have always been upbeat. My mother reminded me that as a young child I always came downstairs in the morning happy—either singing or imitating someone! I had a positive outlook by nature. But now, after many years of reading God's Word, I think I have a hopeful outlook by grace! No matter how turbulent the stock markets or other circumstances get, I know God remains on His throne. I find satisfaction in His unfailing love. My cup is still "full and running over!"

Fourth, most of life's worries are needless— they are false worries.

Let me be frank. I've wasted so much time worrying about things that never happened! Now I look back and wonder what was the point.

Some people are by nature worriers. Some of us are so worried, that in those rare moments we don't worry, we become worried about what we are not worrying about! I am afraid that I am like that.

As a teen I dreamed of being a preacher. But I once witnessed a man named Dr. Walter Wilson preach, and as he spoke his dentures slipped out fell out of his mouth and onto the floor. I watched him pick them up, without missing a word, and put them back in his mouth. Then I feared that I might also lose my teeth!

I remember worrying about losing our home during the Great Depression. Dad put a "for sale" sign in front of the house after he lost his job and we could no longer make the payments. When people came to view the house, we children did not want them to like it, so we would mess things up to make sure they would not want to buy it. Thankfully no one made an offer, except President Roosevelt, who came up with legislation to make it easier for homeowners to keep their house.

In my twenties, when I had cancer, I worried a lot. My doctor told me I might not live. And if I did, he said I would never have children. I suppose that's why I started to live urgently and intensely. I decided I needed to do everything I felt called to do by age 40, because surely I would not live longer than that. When I lived beyond that, and had four kids, I went back to my doctor and asked what happened? He replied, "What do I know?"

Then I worried about my four boys. Would they find their way in life? Who would they marry? After that, I worried about my grandkids. Then I worried about my great-grandchildren!

Now I worry differently. I wonder: Will I have my wits to the end? What if my money runs out? How will I ultimately die?

Then I go to passages like Proverbs 3:5–6 and break them down into four parts and apply it personally. I meditate on that first phrase: "Trust in the Lord with all your heart." Then I go to the next phrase: "and lean not on your own understanding." Then I focus on the words "in all your ways acknowledge him." *All* your ways! Then I rest in that final phrase: "and he will make your paths straight."

This is my SOS verse for the middle of the night when I can't sleep. I keep quoting it so I don't get trapped by false worries. I recite it until I fall back to sleep.

Fifth, God's Word is precious.

Where would I be without it? Throughout my life I have been blessed and strengthened, reproved and made wise by the Bible. As I just illustrated, it remains a lamp to my feet and a light for my path.

It has been the privilege of a lifetime to be able to preach and teach the Word of God. Early on I started teaching the Bible at my childhood church. To this day, by God's grace, I am still preaching occasionally at church and teaching the adult seniors class each Sunday.

The blessings of the gospel, and the "whole counsel of God," are in fact what the Scriptures say they are. "The ordinances of the Lord are sure and altogether righteous. They are more precious than gold, than much pure gold; they are sweeter than honey, than honey from the comb" (Psalm 19:9–10).

I try to communicate this to the younger generation, but I don't know if they understand. They are immersed in a world of more data than any generation in history. Amid all this information I fear they are losing wisdom. They are bombarded by texts every minute. But in the midst of all this texting, they lose sight of the one eternal text inspired by God the Holy Spirit that can make sense of all the others.

I want them to know that, as Isaiah and Peter said, "the grass withers and the flowers fall" (and all the data smog of the digital age will also fall away), "but the word of our God stands forever" (Isaiah 40:8; 1 Peter 1:24–25).

**Sixth, what ultimately counts
is people and living for Christ.**

One benefit of being an octogenarian is that you gain perspective. Because you are somewhere close to the end, you see things more sharply. You have a better sense of what is truly important and what is not.

Let me tell you what is *not* ultimately important. Tomorrow's stock market is *not* ultimately important. Some people spend countless hours poring over the indexes. But in the end, that information is just not all that significant. The state of your garage is *not* all that important.

People spend countless hours tinkering with this or that in their cars. They get lost in games.

The next election is *not* all that important. Well it is, sort of. Elections have great impact. But down the road, this candidate will let you and everyone else down. People will clamor for someone better.

And let me say it loudly: the NFL, the NBA, the NHL, and MLB are *not* that important. Yet people spend an inordinate amount of time getting all worked up about games that do not count.

So what counts? Ultimately only two things: people and what is done for Christ. I will say more about people in a later chapter. People have eternal souls. So obviously, they last. Which is why loving people is very important. Love lasts.

I regret that I've not always been convinced of this. Both of us have been impatient with too many people, blown off too many, and hurt too many.

Veteran pastor John Stott recalls how he had also been slow to learn this lesson. He told of the big challenge of loving those "problem" people in the church. He said you can see them coming when you stand at the door after a sermon. And you want to run in the other direction. Until, he said, you recall how precious they are in the sight of God. They are so valuable as part of the flock of God, because they too have been purchased by the blood of Christ. The Lord has appointed us to be their shepherds.

So he established the discipline of speaking to himself when he would see them coming. He did this to counteract his natural tendency. He would talk to the person silently in his mind and say, "What a precious person you are; it is a privilege to be involved in your care." And the Lord would use this heart-changing reminder to adjust his attitudes.[2]

Along with people, living for Christ is supremely important. It counts so much because Christ is eternal.

When I was young we used to repeat the saying, "Only one life, will soon be passed, only what's done for Christ will last." I still believe that.

My battle with cancer as a young man marked a major turning point in my life. I was forced at an early age to consider things that really mattered. So I imagined my hospital bed as an altar of dedication. In the Old Testament, the priests would take a sacrifice, put the flesh hooks in it, and adjust it to the center of the altar. So at that critical moment, I said to the Lord that I wanted to adjust my life to the center of His will and live for Him, to be a living sacrifice and not squirm off the altar!

That sacred moment became a new beginning for me. It altered the trajectory of my life.

Seventh, life is too short to learn by experience!

These are seven key lessons from my life. Though experience can be the best teacher for some things, life is way too short to learn everything by experience! We can save ourselves a lot of trouble when we learn wisdom lessons the easy way—by listening to the insights of those who have already traveled down the road.

The patriarch Job had a friend named Bildad the Shuhite. While he did not get everything right, one thing he did get right was this. He said, "Ask the former generations and find out what their fathers learned, for we were born only yesterday and know nothing, and our days on earth are but a shadow. Will they not instruct you and tell you? Will they not bring forth words from their understanding?" (Job 8:8–10).

4

RETIREMENT REBELS

The Problem with the Retirement Dream

"THEY WILL FLOURISH IN THE COURTS OF OUR GOD.
THEY WILL STILL BEAR FRUIT IN OLD AGE,
THEY WILL STAY FRESH AND GREEN."
—Psalm 92:13–14

THE BIBLE OFFERS a vision for the second half of life that is much more compelling than the retirement dream so many people hold today. In a nutshell, it is a Psalm 92 vision of the righteous not only being useful but "flourishing" as they age. They have not withdrawn. They are still green and growing. Engaged in service, they bear fruit even in their old age.

Unfortunately, this is not the dream of today's second-halfers. Many Christians have unconsciously adopted America's retirement dream.

What is that dream? It goes something like this. You work until you're 65 (or, if you are really smart, 55), at which time you have amassed enough money so you never have to work again and can spend the rest of your life in leisure. Your motto is like one I saw at a ski resort ad: "Live to play and play to live." You can live off your company pensions and your rising investments, along with a nice Social Security supplement. Then you migrate to somewhere warm—say Florida, Palm Springs, or Arizona—unless you want to take a few years traveling the world or touring the country in your RV. Besides that, you get to watch as much TV as you want, play as much golf as you want, spend all the time on your hobbies that you want, redesign your house as many times as you want, and hang out with your retired friends. That's the good life. A kind of this-worldly paradise.

But there's a problem. In fact there are lots of problems with this dream. That's what this chapter is about.

Do a Google search on your computer and type in, "problem with retirement." Here's what comes up. One problem with retirement is the recent volatility of the stock market. As the market has taken some huge hits, most people have watched their retirement investment accounts plummet.

Also, your company pension is no longer assured. In the latter half of the twentieth century, the corporate perks were starting to fall away. People became less committed to their companies, and their companies were less committed to them. Meanwhile, the value of our homes as a source of equity has also been hit in the Great Recession.

Further, we are living longer. Boomers born in 1955 are expected to live to 79. Which means retirement may last for almost one-third of your life. This also means people may outlive their money. Social Security faces insolvency with 77 million baby boomers about to overload the system, and fewer younger people to support it. But any attempts to alter its structure create a political firestorm.

The bottom line is that this retirement dream is unsustainable. It is falling apart because it simply cannot deliver on its promises. The dream is over, and people need to discover a new vision.

Truth is, the problems associated with retirement are even more complicated than just these issues. So let's explore some of the other problems. But rest assured, the falling apart of one dream offers us an opportunity to rethink the dream and replace it with a better one.

WHERE DID THE RETIREMENT DREAM COME FROM?

It may surprise you that the idea of a universal right to protracted golden years of leisure is fairly recent. In the beginning there was no retirement. Through much of human history, people died early and worked until they died. In 1883, German chancellor Otto von Bismarck invented modern retirement by announcing he would pay a pension to any nonworking German over age 65. He did this to bring new workers into the economy, in order to head off Marxist threats, all the while knowing that few people lived past 65.[1] So it was a safe proposition. Along with this, as the management of work became a science, it was shown that older workers were often less efficient. Their lingering presence in the workforce kept younger, stronger workers unemployed. To reverse this situation, Western governments began to provide incentives to move older workers out and younger, healthier workers in.

The same thing happened in America in the early twentieth century. The Great Depression made the situation even worse. So by the 1930s there were calls proposing mandatory retirement to make room for this younger workforce. The only way to get older workers to stop working was to pay them to stop. This was a basic idea behind the Social Security Act that Franklin Roosevelt put forward in 1935. It was a kind of old age insurance that workers paid into, with retirement at age 65. And with this, a new "age" of retirement was born.

A company pension, your personal savings, and a government Social Security check opened the door to a new stage of life. The rich discovered this leisure first, and by 1910 they started migrating to warm places like Florida. The middle class followed. Retirement communities were created where older people would not see younger people. Between 1920 and 1930, the number of golf courses in America tripled. The advent of movies and television gave those having "nothing to do" another new leisure-time activity.

All this picked up speed after World War II. The vision was to give thirty to forty years to one company, and in return it would pay a good salary and a generous pension. The company you worked for often took care of you.

After a few more decades, retirement as a universal right came into its own all over the Western world, fostered by the entitlement mentality of the modern welfare state.

We have already explained how this whole retirement dream superstructure is falling apart, that it is economically unsustainable. But there are also other problems.

One not-so-obvious problem is that it is a deeply empty way of living. Retirement simply does not satisfy. Golfing as a hobby may be great. But twenty years of doing nothing but putting a little white ball into a hole will grow old fast. A life of only leisure and idleness often leads to boredom, depression, and early death.

Think of it. You get guys who have worked sixty to eighty hours a week for fifty years. Suddenly they retire to have fun. Their hobbies become their mainstay. They spend their days micromanaging retirement accounts, inspecting doctor bills, doing yard work, or tinkering at the tool bench or with the car. We were made to be more productive than this. No wonder study after study shows that complete retirement often means an early trip to the grave. This kind of a life just does not satisfy.

NOT BIBLICAL

The Christian will want to know what the Bible says about retirement. This too is a problem, because the Bible does not conceive of a retirement dream like this.

For starters, the Bible has a much more dignified view of work. Work is not essentially a drudgery to avoid but a God-like activity that can be used for good to bless people. Meaningful work was there at the creation, and it's there at the re-creation of heaven and earth.

Not only that, but the great heroes of the Bible simply do not retire! Consider Abraham. He and his wife served until they were advanced in age. When he was 100 and she was 90, God still had work for them to do. What about Moses? At age 80, he led Israel out of Egypt toward the banks of the Jordan.

And what about those older Levites? Sometimes they are cited as an example of retirement. Numbers 8:23–26 says that at age 50, they no longer had to carry the tabernacle as they traveled. Instead, stronger, younger men were to do the heavy lifting. But this hardly speaks of retirement. The older men still served in various roles in the tent of meeting.

Then there is Caleb. He claimed to be as active and strong at age 85 (according to Joshua 14:10–11), as when he was 45! Rather than seeking ease and retirement, he asked for the enemy-infested hill country so he could drive them out and take it as his inheritance.

Early in the New Testament, we read of Zechariah, a priest who is fully involved in serving the Lord at the temple though he was advanced in years (Luke 1:6–7, 13–17). Luke also mentions two other godly seniors—Simeon and Anna. Simeon, in Luke 2:29–32, is a picture of a senior waiting and serving until his prayer is answered and his dream is realized. Seeing Jesus, he is now ready to depart from this life in peace.

And Anna, an 84-year-old prophetess, is also serving day and night in the temple, according to Luke 2:37. She too is looking for the salvation of Israel.

Nicodemus, in all probability, was a senior leader when we meet him in John 3:1–21. We are not told his age. But he was a ruler of the Jews, and they were older. Not only that, but he responded to Jesus' talk of a new birth by asking, "How can a man be born when he is old?" Yet by the time recorded in John 19:38–42, he advanced from curiosity to bold commitment to Jesus.

Jesus commissioned Peter to follow Him into old age (John 21:18). He and Paul served Christ into their 60s before dying as martyrs. Paul also wrote in Titus 2:2–5 that older men and women were to model the faith and pass it on to younger people.

John the apostle lived well into old age. He not only cared for Mary the mother of Jesus but also pastored the church in Ephesus.

Then late in his life (some say he was over 90), as a prisoner of Rome, he was banished to the penal colony on the island of Patmos. That's when he received the vision that we know as the book of Revelation.

According to reliable tradition, all the apostles, except John, died as martyrs serving Christ to the end. None of them retired with fat pensions at some resort near the Great Sea.

Their lives (as well as the truth of Scriptures like Psalm 92), show that fruitfulness, even late into the second half, is a very real possibility.

It seems then that the biblical ideal for second-halfers is one of usefulness and fruitfulness. Second-halfers don't retire from serving the Lord; they inspire while serving the Lord.

RETIREMENT REBELS I HAVE KNOWN

So why do so many Christians have a retirement view of life? Could it be that our lives are more "squeezed into the world's mold" than we dare admit? (See Romans 12:1–2.) Many of us have bought the retirement dream—hook, line, and sinker.

But not all of us go along. We have known many "retirement rebels," people who have opted out of the retirement dream. They give us far better models.

Some are well known. Think of Billy Graham, serving Christ into his 90s and even then saying he has still not preached his last sermon. Or think of Bev Shea singing into his late 90s.

I think of my friend John Haggai, who carries with him a centenarian Christian vision. He aims to keep serving until age 100. And by God's grace, he will probably do it.

But we've also been inspired by many lesser-known retirement rebels. I think of attorney Doyle Weathers, who immediately after retiring, came to me, saying, "Pastor, I want to serve as an unpaid member of the church staff and help with visitation." Or Johnny Mastry, an attorney from Florida, who "retired" and then served at Reformed Theological Seminary in development. And after that, he went back to school to train as a Christian counselor so he could help other attorneys.

I think of physicians like Chris and Jane Palacas, who left their medical practice in Detroit and sold or gave away their furniture so they could live out their remaining years as medical doctors in Uganda. They bring health care to remote villages, serving vigorously as they approach their 80s.

Another great retirement rebel we have known was Donald Cole, former missionary to Angola and then a prominent radio pastor for the Moody Bible Institute. After years in Christian radio, serving until his 80s, he "took partial retirement" and started going back to Angola as a part-time missionary to give his remaining energies to the church in that war-torn country.

Of course, not everybody can do that. Some second-halfers battle serious health problems that prohibit them from doing many things. But then there are those like Emily Keenan. She and her husband both came to the Lord later in life through Moody radio station WMBI. Not only were they eager to serve others and very generous to Christian ministries, but Emily, after her husband died, committed herself to be a prayer warrior. When she could no longer move around, she would say, "At least I can pray," and committed herself to the ministry of intercession.

I, Don, can also say a word about my dad's example. (He won't.)

I can tell you that he has given many of us a model. After stepping down as president of Moody Bible Institute, he became Moody's chancellor, a grandfather-like role in that ministry. He stepped away from the administrative duties but kept preaching and speaking on Christian radio. Then by his 80s he scaled back a little bit more, no longer traveling and doing radio.

But then he joined the staff of a local church I helped plant in northern Illinois and began serving as director of senior adult ministries, teaching Sunday school weekly, preaching occasionally, and mentoring the senior pastor. In other words, my dad has also been a retirement rebel.

He has occasionally quoted the early twentieth-century baseball player turned evangelist Billy Sunday, who said he wanted to serve the Lord and do battle with the Enemy as long as he lived. But he said it colorfully: "I'll keep beating the devil until my arms fall off, and then I'll kick him until my feet fall off, and then I will bite him until my teeth fall out, and when my teeth fall out, I will gum him 'til I die!"[2]

That, my friends, is the spirit of a Christian retirement rebel. We have heaven and we have Christ, and until the day we die, we're engaged in a spiritual battle that calls for our best energies.

We have heaven. Is that not a whole lot better than the retirement dream? There, our investments and treasures do not lose value. They do not rust or erode with market swings. We will not outlive our pension there, because it has been paid for by Christ.

Have you considered why the retirement dream has so taken hold of the Western world at the same time our culture has become more secular? For many people, retirement is a secular substitute for heaven. When you let go of God and Jesus Christ—and there is no vision of eternal life as we see in the Bible—then this life is all there is.

That's why so many people seek the good life now. Since there is no heaven beyond the grave, they must have it here. So with desperation they hang on to that dream of twenty years in Sun City. The present life is all that exists. And now some of them say it's the government's duty to ensure it is not taken away!

More than sad, this is tragic. It is not a Christian vision. Still, many of us continue to mimic our contemporaries. Perhaps it is because, as John Piper has helpfully reminded us, we do not treasure Christ.

In his little booklet, *Rethinking Retirement: Finishing Life for the Glory of Christ*, Piper gives a charge to aging baby boomers. He calls for a radical break with the mind-set of our unbelieving peers and resolutely resisting what we've called the "retirement dream." We do this, Piper says, by coming back to Christ as our highest treasure, and fighting (a spiritual fight) to delight in Him, persevere in Him, and live every day of our lives to magnify Him.[3]

Retirement rebels understand that we are engaged in a spiritual battle to the end. They know that behind the headlines is the reality of principalities and powers waging war, and evil forces fighting against Christ's kingdom. They know this calls for a vigilant life and a wartime mentality.

I (George) am old enough to remember what it was like to live during World War II. In wartime you live without stuff. Everybody sacrifices for the greater good. Some of us were not on the front lines, but we still wanted to do our part to win the battle. So we lived lean.

Friends, we are living in a day when millions of people are in trouble. Many around the world live without basic food or sanitation and experience great injustices—all of which we should care about. But worst of all, many are without Christ and the hope of the gospel. Meanwhile, if you are reading this book, you not only have access to this treasure, but you also have power to spread the influence of Jesus around the globe. Do you? Will you?

Perhaps it is time to adjust your vision. To trade the old, unsustainable retirement dream for something more Christ-honoring and urgent. Perhaps He is calling you not to withdrawal but to deeper engagement as you grow older—where you serve Him longer, you sacrifice more deeply, and even as your energies begin to decline, you take what you have and live more completely for Him.

The day that first AARP card arrives in your mailbox and reminds you that you are approaching the second half—let that prompt you to become a retirement rebel. Let it be the moment you ask God to renew your mind in this area and shift your vision from personal fulfillment to a Christ-centered vision of serving Him and blessing people in His name, to the very end. Let it move you from retirement to inspire-ment for His kingdom.

Retirement rebel work need not involve vocational ministry. In *The Second-Half Adventure*, Kay Strom points out that baby boomers have excelled in the areas of flexibility, creativity, focus, and organization, abilities that can be put to good use in a variety of ministries.[4] You might put your skills and experience to work in a new field, with new opportunities to serve the people around you. Perhaps you feel God calling you to make the most of your nine-to-five time by visiting people in hospitals, nursing homes, or even in prison. How many grade schools would love to have older adults volunteer each week as an in-class tutor for students from troubled homes? Or instead of volunteer work, you might begin a new career that involves starting a new business that directly helps people. Whether working for justice, feeding the hungry, or serving the poor, when we commit to keep serving God in any way possible, the opportunities are endless.

As I (George) write this, I have in mind a vision of old Herbert Lockyer. When I was a boy, Lockyer was a prominent Bible teacher from Britain. I brought him to preach at the Moody Bible Institute when he was 99 years old. I distinctly remember him. He could not walk well, so he had someone aid him to the platform. Yet in his powerful, low voice, he proclaimed the gospel. I can still hear him. He closed his message by saying, "I am not looking for the undertaker . . . I'm looking for the upper taker." Then he sat down, leaned over to me, and said in his deep voice, "Did I hit the ball out of the park?"

Here was another retirement rebel still bearing fruit in old age. I want to be like that!

5

YOU CAN'T RUN THIS RACE ALONE

Mentors, Friends, and Investing in the Next Generation

"SINCE MY YOUTH, O GOD, YOU HAVE TAUGHT ME, AND TO THIS DAY I DECLARE YOUR MARVELOUS DEEDS. EVEN WHEN I AM OLD AND GRAY, DO NOT FORSAKE ME, O GOD, TILL I DECLARE YOUR POWER TO THE NEXT GENERATION, YOUR MIGHT TO ALL WHO ARE TO COME."
—PSALM 71:17–18

ONE OF THE MEMORABLE moments in recent Olympic history took place in 1992 at the summer games in Barcelona. Like every other Olympian, runner Derek Redmond came to the games with an intense desire to win. At age 19 he had shattered the British 400 meter record. Now he was determined to win the medal in the 400 before the world.

This was not Redmond's first Olympic appearance. He had been forced to withdraw from the 1988 games in Seoul, only ten minutes before the race, because of an Achilles tendon injury. He underwent five surgeries that next year, after which Redmond reemerged as a serious contender. The 1992 Olympics was his time to show the world how fast he was.

Redmond traveled to Barcelona accompanied by his father, Jim. Extremely supportive, Jim tried to come to all of Derek's major races. The two of them were close—so close that when Derek ran, he sometimes felt as if his father were running alongside of him.

On the day of the 400 meter semifinals, Jim watched from the top row of the stadium. When the starting gun fired, 65,000 fans cheered as the runners took off. Early on, Redmond, in lane five, broke from the pack and seized the lead. As he ran, his father cheered with everyone else. With only 175 meters to go, Derek heard a pop. It was his right hamstring. He immediately felt intense pain. Redmond grabbed the back of his right leg and started hopping as the other runners flew by him. Then the British sprinter collapsed in agony.

As the other runners crossed the finish line and the medical unit made its way onto the field, Jim Redmond raced down the stairs. When he reached the bottom row, he knew he had no credentials to be on the track. Yet all he could think about was getting to his son.

Back on the track, Derek realized his dream of an Olympic medal was gone. With tears streaming, as the medical crew arrived with the stretcher, Derek told them, "No, there's no way I'm getting on that stretcher. I'm going to finish my race."

At that moment—one that will never be forgotten by millions of spectators around the world—Redmond lifted himself and started hobbling down the track. In stunned amazement, the crowd began to cheer. Redmond was determined to reach the finish line.

Meanwhile, Jim Redmond got to the bottom of the stands, leaped over the railing, ran past the security guard, and with two more security guards chasing after him, sprinted to his son. "That's my son," he yelled to the guards, "and I am going to help him." The cheer turned into a roar.

When Jim reached his limping son about 120 meters from the finish line, he put his arm around Derek's waist and said, "I am here, son; we are going to finish the race together." The runner put his arm around his father's shoulder and, sobbing, continued. Together, with the crowd going wild, a couple of steps from the finish line, Jim released his grip from his son, so Derek could cross the finish line by himself.

Once he crossed over, Jim threw his arms around his son and said, "I am the proudest father alive. Prouder than if he had won a gold medal."[1]

WE CAN'T DO IT ALONE!

Even those athletes who sprinted across the finish line know that you cannot successfully compete alone. You depend on coaches, trainers, doctors, and friends. But in this instance, it was especially clear that Derek could never have finished the race alone.

The same is true in the long-distance event of the Christian life. In our race, we also need others. To run well, we need mentors and friends.

Some years ago, I (George) remember hearing the extraordinary Dallas Seminary Bible teacher Howard Hendricks speak at a Moody Pastors' Conference. He said that to finish well, every Christian needs a Paul, a Barnabas, and a Timothy. He said we all need a Paul—someone older who can mentor us and show us the way. We all need a Barnabas—someone running alongside to encourage us.

And we all need a Timothy—someone younger, an emerging leader in whom we invest our lives.

Let me tell you about some of those who have been a Paul, a Barnabas, and a Timothy in my life, so you might catch the vision and not try to run the race alone.

WE NEED A PAUL TO MENTOR US

More than anyone, the man who mentored me is someone you've probably never heard of. Pastor Herrmann Braunlin, who lived from 1904 to1995, modeled godliness and servant leadership for me. For a while I served as his assistant at the Hawthorne (New Jersey) Gospel Church. That church was the outgrowth of the crusades that Billy Sunday held in Paterson, New Jersey, in 1924. It started as a Bible study and grew into a gospel mission, then a church, and eventually a megachurch. Herrmann pastored it for sixty-two years. How many people do you know who pastored a church that long?

Lots of things impressed me about my pastor. For one, he was an incredibly hard worker. Before starting at the church, he was a businessman in New York City. He started the church in 1924, serving part-time, then went full-time in 1927. He retired in 1986. I don't believe Herrmann ever took an extended vacation . . . just a few days each year. Back in the 1940s, the expected order for a pastor was God, work, and family. Though no one said it, everyone assumed that work was more important than family.

Early on, the church held summer meetings in a large tent. There were services every night from the last week of June through Labor Day. Herrmann would lead every one of them. Eventually the tent was replaced by a regular church building and also a more permanent pavilion for the summer Bible conference.

Herrmann was part of the IFCA (Independent Fundamental Churches of America), and he even served for a time as its president.

Herrmann Braunlin was a model of truthfulness and grace. Though he encouraged me to join the IFCA, I didn't. I felt that some in the IFCA (though not Herrmann) carried separatism to an extreme. Separation unto Christ—yes. Separation from the spirit of the age—yes. I just could not follow some in the way they separated themselves from other Christians. So I stayed an independent Baptist, and Herrmann still accepted me.

Herrmann also modeled faithfulness and humility. While he had no Bible college or seminary training, Herrmann loved the gospel and was a diligent student of the Bible. He invited guests like Billy Graham, D. Martyn Lloyd-Jones, and A. W. Tozer to preach, and he would say, "I am not an evangelist, so I bring good ones in."

The truth is, he was a gentle soul-winner. He held a ladies' Bible class every Thursday for forty years. He also had a men's Bible class. In both he led many to Christ. He also taught people how to share their faith. This became a permanent feature of his Monday evening school. Herrmann was gentle, solid, and steady in discipling others.

Herrmann was the most self-effacing man I've ever met. Once I said to him, "Herrmann, how come you stayed for sixty-two years in one church?"

He said, "No one ever asked me to leave."

He got few invitations to preach elsewhere. Instead, he plodded along—with careful study and a quiet delivery. He was self-taught yet a solid teacher. He told me that when I taught or preached, I should give my very best every week.

Herrmann was never sensational, but he believed in variety and creativity as he planned programs. Through it all, I never saw him lose his cool, though he easily could have, because he worked with a lot of stubborn people. Every year he invited the church to vote on whether he should continue as their pastor. Every year! He always had at least 7 percent vote against him. Amazingly, that didn't bother him. He said, "George, it's not worth getting upset about, because in all likelihood, I will probably officiate at their funeral services." His philosophy was, if you wait long enough, your congregation changes—20 percent move away in a given year, some will not live long, so you will in effect have a new congregation every year.

Herrmann was also a man of prayer. I can't think of any occasion where we would finish and he would not say, "Can I pray?" Even when I visited him in a nursing home at the end of his life, when his memory was failing, he'd end our meeting by saying, "I want to pray." And he prayed beautifully, because it was his habit all his life. He did this right until the day he died.

The last thing that impressed me about my mentor is that he was a man of unusual vision. Early on, the church met in a small building in the middle of the town. But he led the church to buy ground in a new location, on what was then only a dirt road. His vision was to buy a large acreage and build a regional church with a full-orbed ministry. Eventually that dirt road became a major thoroughfare. The church was in a prime location. And by then it was a multiministry congregation—with a vibrant youth program, strong Bible teaching, an evening school, the largest Christian bookstore in the New York metropolitan area, a missionary home, and a radio ministry. This combination made the church unique.

Today, we would call Herrmann an "entrepreneurial pastor." Often, when I have been faced with a difficult decision, I would ask myself, "How would Herrmann Braunlin handle this?"

I can't imagine what I would have done without having such a dedicated servant of God as my mentor. I was his Timothy, and he was my Paul!

WE NEED A BARNABAS

Besides needing people like Paul in our lives, we also need people like Barnabas. I have been blessed with a number of Barnabas-like friends early in life, who came alongside me, listened to me, and encouraged me. Their encouragement often made the difference and prompted me to go deeper with Christ. Let me tell you about two of them.

One Barnabas for me was Jack Wyrtzen. Jack was known for founding Word of Life camps and Bible institutes all over the world, and for his evangelistic rallies.

Early on, Jack opposed the Christian faith. He went to a Unitarian church and spent much of his time leading a popular dance band. A friend came to share the gospel of John with Jack, but he tore it up. So his friend gave him another. Jack tore that one up too! But one day the Spirit of God got hold of Jack, and he came to faith in Christ. Jack went to Herrmann Braunlin's Hawthorne evening Bible school to get grounded in his faith.

He started holding evangelistic rallies in New York City in the 1930s. Jack was doing what Youth for Christ did, before there was a Youth for Christ. Sometimes he would preach. Other times he would invite the well-known Presbyterian Donald Grey Barnhouse to speak, and Jack would give the invitation. Some of these rallies attracted more than 1,500 young people.

Jack then started radio broadcasts, and the ministry grew. Jack would rent and fill Madison Square Garden for even larger rallies. Billy Graham sometimes preached for him. I preached for him often. Jack had an intense passion for lost people. He would hold evangelistic cruises up the Hudson River. He even rented Yankee Stadium for an evangelistic rally. He did not fill it, but he came close, with hundreds making a profession of faith.

Jack's evangelistic fervor inspired me. He would always challenge me to keep up a daily devotional time in God's Word. This was his practice through his life.

Jack's passion for young people led to the start of the Word of Life camps in upstate New York—the Inn for adults, the Island for teens, the Ranch for kids, and also a family camp. Then he started a Bible school. Word of Life began replicating this pattern overseas. They have started Christian camps and Bible schools all over the world. On my last count, Word of Life had ministries in forty-five countries. Jack's vision inspired me.

Another Barnabas in my life is John Edmund Haggai. Today John is known globally as an inspirational, visionary leader of Christian leaders. His Haggai Institute has trained and discipled many of the top Christian leaders around the world, who, in turn, became Christian influencers.

I met John when we were both students at Moody Bible Institute. John's father grew up in Damascus, Syria, and then fled to the United States. His father and mother graduated from Moody, so John went there as well. That's where we met and became best friends. We have stayed close through the years, talking with each other almost weekly. We'll talk about a text of Scripture, theology, a preacher, a missionary, or some significant issue of the day. John has always enlarged my vision and motivates me to do more than I might have otherwise. John still "winds my clock."

John always had a big vision. He is noted for saying, "Attempt something so great for God it's doomed to failure unless God be in it." Some people thought he dreamed too big.

But John was well informed, walked closely with the Lord, and had boundless energy. He had so much energy he would run circles around others. Besides that, God put a burden on his heart for the souls of Asia. John would say, "I am burdened for Asia. I want to do something for Asia." Some people said he was extreme. Then he launched the Haggai Institute. He even mortgaged his home to start it. His vision was to train nationals and raise up indigenous Christian leadership. He believed this was far more effective in the long run than depending on missionaries from the West. Before others were even talking about this, John was doing it. Before others were talking about raising up ministries overseas that were self-supporting, John was doing that too.

In the early 1960s, he saw the need for a school of evangelism and for the training of an army of international Christian leaders. He wanted to train gifted influencers who would influence their world for Christ. Eventually the Haggai Institute spread beyond Asia. Through the years its graduates have gone on to become corporate leaders or statesmen around the world.

John's lifework is nothing short of extraordinary—and he is still going strong. These are just two of the people who have been a Barnabas in my life. There were more: Larry McGuill, George

Verwer, Jim Gwinn, and others. But time does not permit me to tell you their stories.

THE NEED FOR TIMOTHYS

Besides a Paul and a Barnabas, according to Hendricks, we all need to keep our eye on the younger generation for emerging leaders like Timothy.

Why Timothys? Because they are our future. In the church, they will carry on the work of the gospel long after we are gone. That's why, as a pioneering missionary, Paul poured his life into people like Timothy. When he trained elders, he encouraged them to do the same. He charged Timothy to keep his teaching. Then he added, "And the things you have heard me say in the presence of many witnesses entrust to reliable men who will also be qualified to teach others" (2 Timothy 2:2). Paul had a Timothy and a Titus; do you?

Timothy was a shy young man. People dismissed him because of his youth. He also had stomach problems. But Paul saw his potential and invested in him.

Have you observed, as I have, that many young Timothys fail to finish the race? Many unmentored young pastors drop out, because of disappointment and hardship. They do not have a Paul in their life, encouraging them to keep going and showing the way. They need someone to talk to them about navigating the temptations of life and ministry, about preserving their family and marriage, and about dealing with the sins of lust, greed, pride, hypocrisy, deceit, and judgmentalism. How will they navigate the minefields unless someone lovingly guides them?

Yet, so many leaders I know are too busy for younger emerging leaders. They miss the golden opportunity to invest in a Timothy and thus they waste their wisdom. Don't be one of them.

Today's generation of younger men and women is desperate for older Christian leaders to come alongside them. But they are often intimidated by us and too afraid to ask.

So make the first move.

We believe that mentoring is a critical activity for the second half of life. Ask the Holy Spirit to direct you to a few Timothys. Rather than complain about the younger generation, become an advocate and encourager.

While leading a parachurch ministry like Moody, I sought to not just lead but also to mentor certain individuals on my leadership team. A number of them went on to lead large parachurch ministries themselves (Brandt Gustavson, Jim Gwinn, Mark Sweeney, and Jerry Jenkins, to name a few). I also mentored a select group of others outside of Moody. In my current role at my church, part of my responsibility is to mentor Kerry Bauman, a younger senior pastor.

One person I have seen do this effectively through the years is John Stott. Every few years he would select a study assistant. He did this partly because he needed the help. But he also did so because of a conviction about the future of evangelical church leadership. He wanted to ensure there would be a rising generation of Timothys who would resist the pressures of prevailing culture, stand immovably on the Scriptures, and spend their lives on the gospel.

So John did two things. First, he selected a group of bright young men, which he affectionately referred to as "his apostolic succession." But second, he mentored many young leaders in the developing world, often providing scholarships so they would become trainers of Bible-believing, Bible-studying, Bible-expounding pastors.

Because of watching people like John MacArthur and John Stott do this, I (Don), as a pastor, began to include this as one of my major responsibilities. I knew this would help ensure the stability of a church after I was gone. Some of my mentoring was one-on-one, just hanging out together. Some of it was distance mentoring by regular phone calls and email. Some of it was through group mentoring. Each week I would gather our pastoral team and young pastors for a group I called PIP (Pastors in Progress). Each week we would talk and pray about issues of pastoral ministry and issues facing the church. They learned from me, and their input kept my ministry sharp.

We can't believe how many churches and schools miss this boat. Leaders are too busy, or perhaps they fear sharing responsibility at the senior level. They forget that the younger generation needs to see a living curriculum!

Professional mentoring is not the only way to raise up Timothys. Do you have a family or grandchildren? Talk to your grandchildren each week. See them often. You can have a huge impact on a young person's life in a one-hour conversation. Recently I heard about an older couple who said it was too hard when the kids and grandkids came over because it "interrupted" their routine. Gradually their grandchildren stopped coming. The message got through! Their influence was lost.

Hear the words of the aging psalmist who says, "Since my youth, O God, you have taught me, and to this day I declare your marvelous deeds." Then he adds, "Even when I am old and gray, do not forsake me, O God, till I declare your power to the next generation, your might to all who are to come" (Psalm 71:17–18). He understood the importance of this sacred transmission.

THE HANDOFF IS CRITICAL

In a relay race, the hand off is a critical moment. You can have fast runners on your team, but if you blow the baton pass, you lose it all.

In the 2008 Beijing Olympics, the American men's 4 x 100 relay team had great prospects for winning. But in the qualifying heats, as Darvis Paton extended the baton to his teammate Tyson Gay, the baton fell to the ground and the team was disqualified. That year the women's team was also disqualified for a baton drop at the same spot in the race.[2]

Because of races like this, "dropping the baton" has become a metaphor for a big mistake in life. We can't afford to take this transmission process for granted. In life, we have to be deliberate about investing in the younger generation and ensuring they don't run the race alone.

6

ELEVEN JOBS AND COUNTING

*Becoming Wiser about
Our Transitions and Our Work*

"THEREFORE WE WILL NOT FEAR,
THOUGH THE EARTH SHOULD CHANGE."
—Psalm 46:2 NASB

ELEVEN JOBS! A recent Department of Labor report said that by age 44, the average baby boomer has already held eleven jobs![1] But don't think that trend ends after 50. Face it. The longer we live, the more jobs we will probably have. Which means, for most of us, our work life is far from over. We can expect to have more transitions ahead.

Just how many careers will we have in a lifetime? The most widely cited number is that average US workers will have seven careers. That number is difficult to substantiate, because the US Bureau of Labor Statistics doesn't track lifetime careers like it does jobs. There is no consensus at the bureau on what constitutes a career change.

But they do track the typical American worker's tenure at a particular job, which is currently 4.1 years.[2] Which means Americans go through jobs and careers like they go through automobiles.

DON'T DESPISE YOUR WORK

When second-halfers contemplate the current job instability and their prospects of working longer, it is easy to join in the collective whine that can currently be heard all over the Western world. People riot over this kind of thing! Some despise the fact that they have to work longer.

But Christian second-halfers should see things differently. We bring a different attitude to the workplace. Why? Consider these biblical realities.

The first five words of the Bible proclaim that God is a worker. Genesis 1:1 says, "In the beginning God created." Because God created as He did, the human race was able to flourish. God dignified work by creating, and then delighting in what He had made (Hear the refrain throughout the chapter: "And God saw that it was good").

Not only that, but God created humanity in His image. His first great commission to us was not, "Go into all the world and make disciples." That came later. The first great commission was: Go into all the world to fill and "rule over" it (Genesis 1:28). He appointed us as stewards to work the garden "and take care of it" (Genesis 2:15). In other words, we "image" God when we work and create. All honorable work, no matter how apparently insignificant, offers an opportunity for us to do this.

After the fall, the ground was cursed, but work itself was not. We are still called to magnify our Creator and work for His glory (1 Corinthians 10:31; Colossians 3:23).

The goal of work is not just to make money. It is to glorify God and provide a means for human flourishing.

Do you believe this? If it is really true, then we simply cannot despise work. We might not like a particular job. We might not enjoy the current volatility in the market. But we cannot despise work itself.

OPTIONS AFTER FIFTY

What then should we do in the second half? Perhaps you find yourself secure in a job. You may be secure but antsy and contemplating some kind of change. Maybe you find yourself being squeezed out of a job because of your age. The practice of age discrimination is quite pervasive.

Along with this, the marketplace is changing fast. When the economy contracts in a recession, businesses lay off workers. We've seen a lot of that lately. But that's not the only challenge we face. To reduce costs, more and more companies are outsourcing jobs to other countries. Add to that the digital revolution, which is radically changing the work landscape.

All of this means that second-halfers will have to get smart about finding work, staying current in their jobs, and navigating life's many transitions.

If you're not ready to retire, what are your options? Some will be able to stay where they are. Others will have to step away from one career and retrain for another. This will probably mean cutting back and learning to live on less. It even may involve being uprooted and replanting your family. Some will have to consider bi-vocational or tri-vocational work (doing two or three jobs), pooling various income streams to stay afloat.

BASICS WE DARE NOT FORGET

To navigate the emerging economic landscape, with all its changes, there are two basic things we dare not forget. The first is that we need to hold our positions loosely.

Every job we get is temporary. Every position we hold is a trust. It is given to us. There will come a point where we have to give it back. It is not ours to keep. This is true even if we started the business, even if it was "our idea," even if we think our genius caused the company to exist in the first place.

In the church, we talk in unhealthy ways when we use the pastor's name and say, "I go to Mark's church" or "This is Rick's church." In reality it is neither. It is Christ's church. Pastors are temporary overseers. Every worker is.

Not long ago, I (Don) was invited back to the church where I recently served as senior pastor. I love this church, and I love its new pastor. But this was the first time I had been there under the new pastor's leadership. I came to make a presentation. Some years ago, I got a baseball and invited the two previous pastors to come back and preach. I had each of them sign the ball, and put a reference to their favorite Bible verse underneath. Since I was the church's third pastor, I signed it too. On this Sunday that I returned to the church, I presented the baseball to the new pastor, telling him that the ball belonged not to him but to the manager. We senior pastors are like Major League pitchers. One is the starter. Then comes a middle reliever. Then another. When our time is done, the manager comes out to the mound, takes the ball from us, and we leave the mound. He then gives the ball to the next pitcher.

So on that Sunday, in front of the congregation, I presented the signed baseball to the church's new pastor-pitcher and prayed God's blessing on his ministry. None of us is indispensable except Jesus, the Chief Shepherd. We each have our innings to pitch, but we don't own the mound or the ball.

This is also true in the business world. Which is why it is always wise to hold our positions a little more loosely than we are naturally inclined to do.

A second basic that we dare not forget is this. As second-halfers navigating this new economy, we need to remember the difference between our primary and our secondary calling.

As a Christian, our primary calling is not to hold a particular job title. It is to follow Jesus. Before being called to something, or to somewhere, we are called to Someone. We are called to know, love, and serve the Lord. That is the primary purpose of our life.

It is so natural to define ourselves by the job we now hold. But that is a deadly mistake. Because very soon the position will no longer be ours. Then what?

If you are a Christian and you lose your job tomorrow, you may lose an office and a title, but you have not lost your calling! Your primary identity in Christ remains intact. Were you laid off? Did the business go under? That does not matter. In Christ you are deeply loved. He has called you to be a son or daughter of the new covenant, and you are still called to love, serve, please the Lord, and live for Him—period. Nothing essential has really changed. In fact, you really do not need this job. It is a blip in your life. You have a life apart from it. Your calling preceded the job—and it will outlast the job. Today, you must simply follow Him. As the psalmist put it, you don't need to fear though the earth has changed (Psalm 46:1–3).

God has given you gifts, abilities, and passions. He has put certain things in your heart. In serving Him you will use these in a variety of settings—at home, in a volunteer capacity, or through paid employment.

Along with your primary calling and your gifts, God also gives us secondary callings. He gives us gifts, passions, and assignments. He calls some people to be pastors and missionaries. He calls some to homemaking. He calls some to music, others to architecture, teaching, food distribution, manufacturing, design, counseling, hospitality, development, engineering, information technology, law, politics, caring for the land, sales, health care, banking, starting businesses, etc. These are all honorable callings where we can glorify God and help people flourish.

Secondary callings are particular career areas where we use our unique passions and gifts to serve Him. They are secondary, not because they are inferior but because they gain their meaning in relation to our primary calling. Your primary calling is to know, love, and serve the Lord. But let's say that God has given you a deep love for nature and the land. You are not just a passionate outdoorsman but feel a deep responsibility for being a good steward over creation. And let's say He calls you to the field of wildlife conservation or land management. That is your secondary calling. You serve the Lord through these interests and passions. It is an honorable way to serve Him.

Along with these callings, we also have our particular jobs. We can serve God in our primary and secondary callings in many different jobs and locations. When we change jobs, our calling remains. Likewise, when we step down from one job, we do not lose our gifting. We simply switch the place where we live these out.

We believe that God calls us in these primary and secondary ways. But we also believe that He calls us to particular jobs and places, even though there is much mystery about how this actually works.

He calls some of us to serve Him in New Jersey, some in Illinois, some in California, some in Colorado, and some in Florida. How do we know? Because each of us has lived in and been called to one of these places. Sometimes He calls us to serve Him cross-culturally or in other countries. He calls some to serve Him in China, India, Great Britain, Venezuela, the Czech Republic, Uganda, etc. These too are His assignments.

But even Christians tend to reverse the order in which we place these things. The biggest mistake people usually make is to see our job as everything and forget about our calling. A job is not everything. It is merely a job—a special, temporary assigned place to live out our love for Him. But there is much more to life than one job.

Do you live as a called person? Or are you just doing a job? If you haven't thought about this in the first half of your life, the second half provides you a wonderful opportunity to start anew.

NAVIGATING THE TRANSITIONS

With these basics in mind, how do we make transitions? How do we know when it is time to step away from one thing—and where to go next?

A woman came up to me recently and said, "I am thinking of retiring and starting the second half of my life. What should I do?" That same day a man told me his job was soon to be eliminated. He had trained as an engineer and worked for the space industry in Florida.

When the government abruptly shut down the manned space program, it caught a lot of people off guard. As in other industries, thousands of jobs are being eliminated. What should he do?

Let's think about that for a moment.

Listen

After you are clear about your callings and your gifts, it is important to listen. Transitions go better when we practice a double listening. First, listen to those around you who know you well. That may be your parents, your spouse, your friends, or your colleagues. Ask them where they think your strengths lie. Where do they think you would thrive? And where wouldn't you thrive? Ask them to be honest—and respect their response.

Ask where they think you can be the most useful for your Lord and master. Puritan Richard Baxter said, "Choose that employment or calling (so far as you have your choice) in which you may be most serviceable to God. Choose not that in which you may be most rich or honorable in the world; but that in which you may do the most good, and best escape sinning."[3]

Second, listen to the Holy Spirit speak to you. We believe that God speaks clearly when we are listening to Him through His Word. While both of us are firm believers in the "take out a sheet of paper and list the pros and cons" method of evaluation, we think there is something more important than that. That is where, with an open Bible, a pencil, and a journal, we listen to God speak through the Bible over a season of weeks or months—and then look for patterns to emerge in our listening, where we clearly discern the mind of the Spirit for our lives.

Watch

Besides listening, we must "watch." Watch the providential circumstances of your life. We believe that God guides the events of our lives. He rules the world by His providence. He is in control of the things that happen to us. So . . . what is happening? Are doors opening or shutting? Is there fruitfulness in your work? Is your team working together? Are key relationships healthy or are they ruptured? Is the wind filling your sails, or are there intractable problems?

We are not simply asking if there are problems. Problems, trouble, and conflict are a part of any job. Handled wisely, they provide opportunities to grow and go forward. But there is a kind of problem that can be lethal to staying in a job.

Check some of the leading indicators of your life. One indicator is performance reviews. How are they going? We all need good feedback. Wise leaders allow themselves to be evaluated.

A second indicator is our own personal motivation. Are you motivated to serve there—or has your enthusiasm dropped off? Do you have patience and love for the people you serve? Attitude shifts may be a sign that something is not right.

A third indicator to watch is your energy level. I (George) felt fatigue toward the end of my ministry at Moody. After so many years, I simply did not have the energy I used to. My enthusiasm for the work was not as great. I used to say, "Don't put off until tomorrow, what you can do today." But I found myself saying, "Don't do today, what you can put off till tomorrow!" That was not good! That's when I made the shift from president to chancellor.

There are things you can do to sustain your energy in the second half. One amazing discovery of smart second-halfers is the afternoon nap! I think of British prime minister Winston Churchill's famed midday siesta. As he grew older, it became a nonnegotiable part of his day. He found that if he took a serious nap each day, he could accomplish two days of work in one day, increasing his alertness and creativity. He said it was the key to his success in leading his country through the Battle of Britain![4]

A fourth indicator is our sense of God's assignment for us. When I (George) went to Moody as president, I did not plan to stay more than fifteen years. I told the board that. They wanted me to stay through the Institute's 100th anniversary, so I stayed on as president until my sixteenth year. After that, they still wanted me to stay. But I felt as if I had completed that particular assignment. I believe this was an inner conviction given to me by the Holy Spirit. Then a new role opened up for me as chancellor.

When it was publicly learned that I would step down as president, several outstanding offers came to me from other ministries. But I was committed to helping Moody Bible Institute complete its Century II plan, which included a top-of-the-line library and educational building, as well as a state-of-the-art physical fitness center. At that point I became chancellor. In that role I had the time to help these two buildings become a reality by raising the necessary funds. I was convinced this was God's assignment for me.

As you check these leading indicators, you start to know on the inside what is the right thing to do—even if others are telling you to do something different.

Learn

Don't stop learning. We've met too many people who think that learning and schooling are only for the first half of life. Not anymore. Many second-halfers are going back to school. There are two main age groups among today's seminary students. There's the under-thirty crowd at the beginning of their career. But now there is a growing over-fifty crowd, the second-halfers, who are retooling.

In this economy you can't stop learning. A digital economy requires that you get up to speed. I (George) have never learned to use a computer. I've written books and led large institutions, but that was mainly in a precomputer age. That won't work in today's world.

Don't wait for someone to come along and hand a job to you on a silver platter. Figure out what you need to learn—and learn it so you are ready for the next opportunity.

Business writer Tom Peters puts it starkly when he says that in today's economy you have to "be your own brand" or "be your own CEO."[5] Because more people are freelancing, you have to figure out how to distinguish yourself from others and create a distinctive role for yourself. Now more than ever, workers need to learn, improve, and build up their skills.

One does not have to adopt Tom Peters's excessive individualism to benefit from his point. You must diversify and deepen your skill set so you can keep going and extend your shelf life and impact in today's marketplace.

Rest

A final thing to keep in mind as you navigate transitions is resting in the Lord. Having done all you can do to prepare yourselves for working in the second half, you can rest in God's sovereignty and grace, knowing He is there to guide you. Ephesians 2:10 says "For we are God's workmanship, created in Christ Jesus to do good works, which God prepared in advance for us to do." Each of us, saved by His wonderful grace, are His unique and special creative work, "poems with a purpose," as some have said. We are designed in our union with Christ Jesus to accomplish those things in life that God has planned for us to do!

This is a precious truth for those who live in an "eleven jobs and counting" world. God is in charge! Trust Him. Rest in Him. He has planned our lives and our works. He gives assignments. He changes assignments. He is there to catch us when we step down and step out in faith into a new role.

7

PACESETTERS

Friends Ahead of Us
Who Have Gone the Distance

"THEREFORE, SINCE WE ARE SURROUNDED BY SUCH
A GREAT CLOUD OF WITNESSES, LET US THROW OFF
EVERYTHING THAT HINDERS AND THE SIN THAT
SO EASILY ENTANGLES, AND LET US RUN WITH
PERSEVERANCE THE RACE MARKED OUT FOR US."
—HEBREWS 12:1

"REMEMBER YOUR LEADERS, WHO SPOKE THE WORD
OF GOD TO YOU. CONSIDER THE OUTCOME OF THEIR
WAY OF LIFE AND IMITATE THEIR FAITH."
—HEBREWS 13:7

SALLY ROBBINS WAS a member of Australia's rowing team in the 2004 Olympics. But something went terribly wrong for her team as they competed in the women's eight final. With 400 meters left in the race, the 23-year-old suddenly stopped rowing! She slumped over and her oar sunk into the water, breaking the synchronized stride needed to win a race. Australia dropped from third to last place in the event. Said Robbins, "I just rowed my guts out in the first 1,500 and didn't have anything left, and that's all I could have done for today." Her teammates were not impressed and neither were the Melbourne newspapers. When Robbins quit the race, she cost the team their medal.[1]

Over the years you will meet lots of people who give up before the race is over. They quit. That's true in just about every human endeavor. You even find it in the Bible. Scripture mentions about a thousand leaders. Of those, about one hundred are very prominent. Still, we have enough information on only about half of them to assess how they finished. And of that number, it appears that only 30 percent finished well.[2]

Look around and you are bound to be discouraged by many who do not go the distance. We've seen many who have fallen, failed, or fizzled. But thankfully, that's not the whole story.

The writer of Hebrews refers to individuals who are now part of that "great cloud of witnesses." In their lives, they lived by faith and did not quit. They are there to inspire us as we run our race. He calls us to remember our leaders, to consider the outcome of their faith, and to imitate what they did right.

In this chapter I want to introduce you to three pacesetters in our lives who've inspired us. They all happen to be nonagenarians —people who lived into their tenth decade. Think of it, ten decades! Both of us have spent time with them. Their names, you probably know.

BILLY GRAHAM

I (George) first met Billy back in 1945 after he preached at a Youth for Christ rally at the Moody Church. It was the beginning of a lifelong friendship. Back in those days, he was not famous. He was, like myself, a young evangelist, traveling around the country, telling people about Jesus. A lot of water has gone under the bridge since then. Now Billy Graham is recognized as the man who has preached the gospel to more people than anyone else in history. He has preached to hundreds of millions in more than 180 nations. It is estimated that millions have made commitments to Christ as a result of his worldwide ministry.

William Franklin Graham was born in 1918 on a farm near Charlotte, North Carolina. He came to faith in Christ under the preaching of Dr. Mordecai Ham in 1934. After some years of training, he became a pastor, a college president, and then an evangelist with Youth for Christ.

In the 1940s he started holding evangelistic rallies on his own. But it was his twenty-five-day 1949 Los Angeles crusade, which drew over 350,000, that brought him to the nation's attention.

In 1950 he founded the Billy Graham Evangelistic Association and began holding three evangelistic campaigns a year. In 1951 he began broadcasting *The Hour of Decision* on radio and television. In 1956 he launched the magazine *Christianity Today.* He is known for mass evangelism and campus evangelism, as well as newspaper, magazine, radio, TV, movie, and Internet evangelism. He has authored many books. Along with Harold John Ockenga, Carl F. H. Henry, Vernon Grounds, and others, Billy became one of the leaders of the neo-evangelical movement in America. This movement tried to distinguish itself from the growing negativity and separationism of the fundamentalist movement. Instead, it called for a more culture-engaging, positive, and socially responsible evangelicalism.

Billy was at the center of virtually every major event of evangelical Christianity during the second half of the twentieth century —including the initiation of global conferences on evangelicalism in Montreux (1960), Berlin (1966), Lausanne (1974), and Amsterdam (1983, 1986, and 2000), and the Lausanne Congress on World Evangelism in 1974 and its follow-up meetings in Manila (1989) and Cape Town (2010)!

I (George) had friends who urged me to separate from Billy because of his cooperation with some mainline church leaders. But I wouldn't, because I believed that God had His hand on Billy's life and was using him mightily (even though I did not always agree with everything he did or said).

Some accused me of apostacizing for supporting him. I participated in his crusades and congresses. He would sometimes speak for me at Moody Church and Moody Bible Institute.

Here are some of the things that impress us most about Billy Graham.

1. *He had immense leadership gifts.* Most people think of him only as a great evangelist, but he was also a great leader. Someone said, "To work for Billy Graham is to grab a strap, pray, and hang on!"[3] He led a large, well-oiled organization. He raised money, enlisted people, and initiated visionary projects. But he had a great team around him and could delegate. Despite the great team, he was still the undisputed leader.

2. *For all his success, he maintained a basic humility and exhibited a servant style of leadership.* Billy found time to do small favors for ordinary people. He had the wisdom to have close friendships with ten presidents and was sharp enough

to survive fifty years of the press. Yet he went to great lengths to praise and promote others. And the older he got, the more there was a prayerfulness about Billy Graham. Prayer and dependence upon the Holy Spirit became central to all the crusades. One key criterion for accepting an invitation for a crusade was the level of prayer support in a city. Without that as a foundation, he believed little could be accomplished spiritually.

3. *Billy was intensely focused.* He said, "I'll go anywhere to talk to anybody about Christ."[4] That included churches, rock concerts, talk shows, pubs, and the world's trouble spots like Vietnam, North Korea, and South Africa. People tried to get him to take detours—to invest in land, go into acting, and become an ambassador. President Lyndon Johnson even urged him to run for president. But Graham replied, "God called me to preach, and I'll never do anything else as long as I live."[5]

4. *He stuck to the simple gospel message.* Billy once said, "When I preach the Bible straight—no questions, no doubts, no hesitations—then God gives me a power that's beyond me. When I say, 'the Bible says,' God gives me this incredible power. That's something that I don't completely understand. When I pick up the Bible, I feel as though I have a rapier in my hands."[6] So he preached ordinary sermons. But the theme was always the same—God's redemptive love for sinners through the cross and the need for personal repentance and faith.

5. *His life was marked by integrity.* Graham's personal integrity and that of the Billy Graham Evangelistic Association team, especially in financial matters, set an example that earned

him the respect and admiration of many. He understood
early on that three of the most common pitfalls of ministry
are pride, financial abuse, and sexual immorality. So he and
his team entered into a pact, known as the Modesto Manifesto, resolving to uphold high standards in each of these
areas. They determined that integrity would be the hallmark
of their ministry.

In citing these characteristics, I do not mean to overlook Billy's
self-professed shortcomings—being away from his family too
much, succumbing to partisan politics in a way that diluted his
evangelistic impact, and being used by politicians. Nor do I wish
to minimize the great challenges he faced—all kinds of health problems, the loss of privacy, multiple threats on his life and family, and
Parkinson's disease.

But in the end, at 93 years and counting, this beloved brother
has been steadfast to his calling as an evangelist and preacher of
the gospel of Jesus Christ. He wants to be remembered as "a man
who was faithful to the Lord and who put Christ first." It looks as
if he is on track.

JOHN STOTT

Of these three pacesetters, I knew John Stott the least. Don knew
him best. I first invited him to speak at Moody in the 1970s. Don
later went on to work on his board—the Langham Foundation, John
Stott Ministries, and the Langham Partnership International.

Billy Graham called British pastor John Stott "the most re-
spected clergyman in the world today."[7] Biographer John Pollock

described him as "in effect the theological leader of world evangelicalism."[8]

John Stott was born in 1921 in London. After training at Rugby School and Cambridge, he was ordained into the Anglican ministry and served at one church, All Souls, Langham Place, in London for more than sixty years (as curate, rector, and then rector emeritus).

As an urban pastor, Stott set forth a model for international city-center ministry that was rooted in five things: the priority of prayer, expository preaching, regular evangelism, careful follow-up, and systematic training of leaders. To this was added another conviction, that the loving service that God sends His people into the world to render includes both evangelism and social action, each as an authentic expression of love.

It was Stott's influence, more than any other, that led to the resurgence of postwar British evangelicalism. Before he became known for his global ministry, he played a key role as a leader of Anglican evangelicalism, leading the National/Evangelical Anglican Congresses, the Church of England Evangelical Council, British Scripture Union, and the British Evangelical Alliance. Stott also gave himself to evangelizing students through university missions and equipping future Christian leaders through UCCF (Universities and Colleges Christian Fellowship). In all of this he had a passion to relate God's timeless Word to the contemporary world. On six occasions he served as the Bible expositor for the triennial Urbana Student Missions Convention.

Stott was an articulate spokesman for biblical and evangelical Christianity in our generation, proclaiming and defending evangelical truth in formative statements, books, sermons, and lectures.

He was the pen behind the Lausanne Covenant (1974) and the Manila Manifesto (1989). He was the author of some forty books, which include *Basic Christianity* (one of the most successful Christian books of the twentieth century), *Christian Basics, Your Mind Matters,* The Bible Speaks Today commentary series, *The Cross of Christ, I Believe in Preaching, Issues, The Contemporary Christian,* etc. He has provided a model of thoughtful Christianity as he sought to apply the Word, yet build a bridge from the text to the modern world.

When he became rector emeritus at All Souls in 1970, John Stott began traveling more—with a strategic focus on equipping and mentoring pastors in the "Majority World." As he traveled, he discovered that liberal foundations in the West were providing scholarships to train developing-world students at liberal Western seminaries. This was damaging the cause of the gospel in their countries. So he was led to start a countermovement to promote biblical orthodoxy in the Majority World. He set up the Evangelical Literature Trust, largely funded by his own book royalties, to send theological books to pastors and teachers.

Then he started the Langham Foundation (which took hold in many countries under different names, but internationally is now known as the Langham Partnership International) to provide scholarships for intellectually able evangelical scholars from developing nations to earn their doctorates and then return to their own countries to teach in theological seminaries. This strategic global vision was needed to help shape the phenomenal church growth of the "new Christendom." The end goal for Stott was to plant pastors in the global South and East who "sincerely believe, diligently study, faithfully expound and relevantly apply the Word of God."[9]

Like each of the pacesetters described in this chapter, John Stott was not without his shortcomings. He could be abrupt and exacting at times. Some American evangelicals dismissed him because of his break with D. Martyn Lloyd-Jones over the issue of remaining in the Church of England, or for his view on annihilationism. While both of us disagree with him on that point, it is a mistake to overlook the huge effect that John Stott has had on the worldwide evangelical movement.

What impressed us most about John Stott was his friendly, courteous, and disarming humility. This came through whether he was interacting with students or famous scholars. For all he achieved, John Stott still thought of himself as one who leaned wholly on the grace of God, who trusted in the righteousness of Christ, and who was an unworthy servant of his Master. He modeled a life of faithfulness and integrity as a humble partner with fellow Christian leaders around the world. John Stott was another pacesetter who modeled long-distance Christianity.

VERNON GROUNDS

A third nonagenarian friend who has gone ahead of us, did not quit, and is now part of that great cloud of witnesses is Vernon Grounds. Dr. Grounds was a pastor, scholar, preacher, counselor, mentor, and evangelical statesman who racked up more than seventy years of ministry.

Not only was Dr. Grounds one of the founders of the American evangelical movement, but he also served with distinction at Denver Seminary for more than sixty years in positions ranging from academic dean, to president, to chancellor. In all, he modeled a firm faith with a kind spirit.

Vernon and his wife, Anne, were longtime family friends. He was born in 1914 and grew up near us in northern New Jersey. He knew all my (Don's) grandparents. And he taught in the Hawthorne Evening Bible School started by Herrmann Braunlin.

In 1950, Grounds moved west with the dream of helping grow a new Conservative Baptist seminary in Denver, now known as Denver Seminary.

In the 1950s and early '60s, Vernon Grounds was one of the leaders of the neo-evangelical movement that emerged out of American fundamentalism. Along with theologians like Carl F. H. Henry, he pointed out some of the blind spots in the fundamentalist movement. Early on, he made a clear case for the importance of social action and care for the poor (see his book *Evangelicalism and Social Responsibility*).

Grounds was a loving critic of fundamentalist Christianity. He would say that it was sometimes "too little fun, too much damn, and too little mental!" While he shied away from its separatist tendencies, he was quick to insist that he was a fundamentalist theologically—he believed in the fundamental teachings of Christianity. He reminded students that fundamentalism, in the original meaning of that term, was about the defense of the gospel in a life-and-death struggle with liberalism, which denied the essential truths of the Bible.

But Grounds pointed out that in many quarters, fundamentalism sometimes degenerated into quarrelsome bickering over incidentals. He said that its all-too-common legalistic pharisaism lacked a "Calvary love." In an incisive critique written in *Eternity* magazine, entitled "Is Love in the Fundamentalist Creed?" Grounds said that the critical flaw of fundamentalism was its lovelessness—an ungracious, sometimes negative, and narrow outlook on life that seemed to undermine the gospel it defended.[10] So he sought to build a seminary campus that represented a vibrant, yet biblically rooted evangelicalism that was true to the gospel and marked by academic excellence, brotherly love, and a social conscience. In so doing, he helped change the face of evangelical Christianity in America, even though some severely criticized him for not being more militant and separatistic.

As an educator, Vernon Grounds repeatedly reminded seminary students that they could love God deeply by studying hard. We are to love the Lord with all our heart and with all our minds, he would say. Dr. Grounds also emphasized that a Christian community, like the seminary, must be characterized by a brotherly love as reflected in the second great commandment to love our neighbors.

Vernon Grounds was a lifelong Baptist. Although he almost went to Westminster Theological Seminary, he enrolled instead at Faith Theological Seminary, founded by Carl McIntire. Still, he took away a classical seminary education in the Reformed tradition. I (Don) can remember a few times when he would visit our church. He would tell me how much he loved the music and service, then say something like, "Well brother, almost thou hast persuadest me to become a Presbyterian!"

Dr. Grounds was always thoughtful, having a lifelong fascination with philosophers, psychologists, and theologians. He himself traveled through a season of doubt and skepticism as a student. His faith was awakened in a youth revival on the East

Coast in the late 1930s. From that time on, one of the themes of his life was the good news of God's love in Jesus Christ. This shaped his personality, for he was characterized by a genuine humility and an authentic and gracious love for people.

While Vernon Grounds was a scholar, he was also an effective counselor, promoting the place of Christian counseling in the evangelical world at a time when many dismissed it as a worldly enterprise. He took a pastoral interest in students, mentoring many, and was an encourager to local pastors like myself.

When I (Don) came to Denver twelve years ago, Dr. Grounds was one of the few people I knew. Along with my father, he spoke at my installation service at Cherry Creek Presbyterian Church. He was a regular source of wise advice. When Christina and I got stuck in our marriage, it was Dr. Grounds whom we turned to for help. He was an effective and fair listener, and with the Spirit's wisdom he could always point the way forward.

There are two things we most admire about Vernon Grounds. One, he never retired from ministry. Almost to the end of his life, he made daily trips to his seminary office to meet with students. He kept involved in a reading group with friends and professors. While residing in an assisted living home, he pastored that community. When he moved to Wichita, he looked forward to ministry opportunities there—at age 96! Dr. Grounds never stopped serving. He was also a good steward of his body—though often attributing his long life to the three Gs: God, genes, and the gym (where he would work out regularly).

The other thing we admire about Vernon Grounds is the legacy of faithfulness he has left for so many of us. His life story is recounted in the biography by Bruce Shelley, *Transformed by Love: The Vernon Grounds Story*.

Like Billy Graham and John Stott, he is another one of those Christians who have gone the distance with Christ—a pacesetter. While these men are all too human, we are right to call them godly men, because of their extraordinary nonagenarian "long obedience in the same direction." They were all giants, but they all knew that they desperately needed a Savior—and ably commended Him to others.

8

YOU CAN'T TAKE IT WITH YOU WHEN YOU GO

"WHOSE WILL THEY BE?"
— LUKE 12:20 ESV

MOST STUDENTS we know are in a season of accumulation. Some are married with growing families. They need more furniture. They need more space. They are also buying more books. Since many of these students will be pastors, accumulating books and study tools is important.

Books are a key part of a pastor's workshop. Pastors need an adequate personal library to help them direct a church, study the Bible, and think through all kinds of issues. Just as a first-rate carpenter needs excellent tools for his craft, so pastors also need a thoroughly equipped tool bench. Blessed are the churches that give their pastors a book-buying budget so they can have a set of first-rate tools for their craft.

Most people who live in a season of accumulation are not collecting books, but other things. That probably includes furniture, a house, a car, a second car, and whatever other collectables or life treasures happen to turn them on.

Lately I (Don) had the privilege of spending time with some senior saints nearing the end of their public ministries. Each of them reminded me of the limits of accumulation.

It started a few years ago with my own father. Through the years I always admired my dad's study, filled with all kinds of books. A number of years ago he was talking about downsizing and giving away about a third of his library. I thought, *Dad, you can't give away all those precious books!* To me it was a very sad moment, because his study was an extension of himself. Still, I understood that at his age and stage, it was appropriate to begin scaling back. It also forced me to think about my possessions.

Not long after that, I had the privilege of spending time with another senior saint after he ended his public ministry. At this time Roger Nicole was living in an assisted living facility in central Florida.

Roger was professor emeritus of theology at Reformed Theological Seminary (RTS) in Orlando. He was a native Swiss Reformed Baptist theologian—a graduate of the Sorbonne in France, Gordon Conwell, and Harvard. Roger Nicole has been long regarded as one of the preeminent theologians in America. Roger earned not one but two doctoral degrees! He was a founding member and past president of the Evangelical Theological Society, and authored or coauthored countless articles and fifty-plus books. Roger once had a massive library with many rare books. Several years ago he gave a large portion of that library to the seminary. RTS now houses the Roger Nicole collection.

I recently discovered that when Dr. Nicole was just starting his teaching career at Gordon College in the 1940s, my dad was a student there and knew him. So now, more than a half-century later,

I was visiting him at the end of his teaching career, and I was his president!

Go figure!

When I last saw him, just before he died, Dr. Nicole was also in his midnineties. While he couldn't hear well, his mind was extremely sharp. In our conversation he kept speaking about life's "retrenchment." Do you know the word? It is often used of organizations. The word refers to a reduction in costs or spending in response to an economic downturn. But used more generally, it refers to reducing something, scaling back, downsizing.

Roger told me about the way God had blessed his life. But now, he said, he was in a season of retrenchment. On the day of our visit, he was particularly miffed because he was allowed to bring only 150 of his books into his assisted living room. Then he went on to tell me about the other things he has given up. "I don't have classes anymore" (it was plain he missed his students). He added, "And I don't have Annette anymore" (his beloved wife who had died several years ago). Then he spoke of losing some of his abilities; his hearing loss bothered him most.

Encounters with a senior saint like this can be wonderfully instructive. For while this retrenchment business may not be our present experience, it soon will be. There is wisdom in occasionally looking down the road. We envision ourselves losing a career, then a house, our driving privileges, and our health.

It is so easy to define ourselves by our stuff. Students building their libraries do so in their season of accumulation. Educators enjoy the pleasures of being surrounded by our books and take pride in our libraries. Every weekend the newspaper is full of ads trying to get us to buy more.

Roger's emphasis on retrenchment was a one-word warning to second-halfers that, sooner or later, we will all experience the stripping away of all we have. Scripture reminds us, "We brought nothing into the world, and we can take nothing out of it" (1 Timothy 6:7). As the old country music song exclaimed, "You can't take it with you when you go." Sooner or later you have to give it away.

In Luke 12 we find the parable of the rich fool. A man comes to Jesus and asks Him to command his brother to divide their family's inheritance. Jesus was reluctant to resolve this dispute, but He took the occasion to speak with them about how they handle their possessions. So He interrupts their conversation to tell them to be on their guard against all covetousness.

"One's life," He said, "does not consist in the abundance of his possessions" (Luke 12:15 ESV). At this point He tells them a story about a rich man whose land produced a great crop. The harvest was so great that he ran out of storage space. "What shall I do?" he thought. He then decided that he must build bigger barns. He would store all his produce, and then tell himself to relax, to eat, drink, and be merry, for he had ample goods laid up for many years.

Different temptations hit particularly hard in each phase of life. The great sin of youth is lust. In the years when our hormones are flowing, this is often an area of great enticement. While it is not the only temptation, it tends to be dominant.

The great sin of middle age is power or pride—the self-sufficient drive that says, "I can do it on my own, and in my own way, and I do it for me."

But the great sin of old age is usually greed or covetousness. We accumulate and never feel we have enough. What we do have, we do not want to let go.

This insecurity of never having enough is endemic to old age, but it may also be generational. Those of us who grew up during the Great Depression have a drive to make sure we have enough. We are still reacting to a childhood of scarcity and have carried that with us all through life. We keep wondering if "we're going to make it." It's amazing how many people we know who think that way. Yet when we die, it turns out that we have more than enough.

Sometimes I hear wealthy friends tell me how frugal they are. They will say they drive a used car, iron their own shirts, or bypass Starbucks for the coffee at McDonald's! But they usually practice a *selective* frugality. They often live in extraordinary neighborhoods and have multiple homes or very expensive hobbies. Yet in certain areas they are in fact very frugal. That is one reason they became wealthy in the first place. Still, they have so much.

What's your attitude toward things? As we see in this parable, one of the inclinations in the second half of life is to worry about security, to grasp and to stockpile. Many of us hold and store much. We may not have barns, but our closets, basements, and garages are full.

The rich man in Jesus' parable made two false assumptions. First, he counted on having many years—which he didn't. His life was about to abruptly end. Second, he supposed he could hang on to his stuff, which he couldn't. God said, "Fool! This night your soul is required of you, and the things you have prepared, whose will they be?" (v. 20). The answer: not yours! They will pass into someone else's hands within the next twenty-four hours.

The man was stingy. He was keeping things to himself. Covetousness had conquered his heart. He was not generous, and he was not rich toward God.

If you haven't noticed, the parable commends generosity.

Why? Several reasons. First, it commends generosity for the simple reason that we can't keep what we own. We can't take it with us when we die. As the old country hit by Ricky Skaggs goes, "All the treasures in this world don't mean a thing when they lay ya low, 'cause you can't take it with you when . . ." Go ahead. Finish the refrain.

Why else? Because generosity breaks the power of greed and frees our heart from covetousness. Holding our possessions tightly endangers our faith. It constantly tempts us to transfer our trust from God to riches. Luke's gospel contains many warnings on this. The history of Israel, as seen in Deuteronomy 8, illustrates the truth of this. When Israel was blessed, it started to trust in the blessings and not the giver of blessing. After prospering, their hearts were "lifted up" and they forgot the Lord. They focused on the blessing and not the blesser. They eventually pursued wealth as an end in itself. It became an idol. The longer and tighter you hold on to your possessions, the more covetous you get.

Why else does the parable commend generosity? Thirdly, because riches laid up in heaven are the most secure. They truly last. D. L. Moody once met with a wealthy farmer. Boasting, the farmer said, "Everything you can see for miles is mine. Look to the south. Look to the north. It's all mine."

Moody pointed to heaven. "How much do you have in that direction?"

When we are rich toward God, what we have can never be taken away. That is why we encourage people to give generously to their local churches, to schools like Moody and RTS, and to Christ-honoring ministries and missionaries who are representing Christ all over the world. Businesses often will not give to gospel-focused ministries. Corporations will not give them grants. The government will not give them aid. They don't rely on mega-billion-dollar endowments like Harvard. Unless God's people support them, they have to close shop!

Why else does generosity matter? Because today we have control over our treasures—but tomorrow we may not. Jesus said, the things you have prepared, tomorrow "whose will they be?" (Luke 12:20 ESV).

When you are gone, will your children and grandchildren value what you value? Will they share the same Christian commitment? I hear many Christian family foundations wonder about this privately. They worry about the possibility of the next generation forgetting God—that their interest will shift from Christian things to social things, perhaps to anti-Christian things. Their worries are legitimate.

It's been said that when wealth comes to a family, the first generation makes the money by discipline, hard work, and often with the desire to honor God. The second generation enjoys the benefits of the money but do not necessarily value what the parents valued. The third generation takes the money for granted and often loses it, or uses the money in ways that would cause their grandparents to roll over in their graves. How many foundations were started by conservative people whose heirs have diverted the money to liberal causes? It takes only three generations to destroy a family enterprise.

That is why I (George) have often told older people, "Do your giving while you're living . . . because then you're knowing where it's going!"

It is a long-known principle that when wealth is tightly held, it waters down faith. In the Middle Ages some monks put it this way: "Discipline begets abundance; abundance, unless we use the utmost care, destroys discipline." Evangelist John Wesley put it his way: "I fear, wherever riches have increased, the essence of religion has decreased in the same proportion!"[1] Religion, he believed, must necessarily produce industry and frugality, and these produce riches. But as riches increase, so does pride, anger, and love of the world. American Puritans like Cotton Mather put it this way in speaking of his beloved New England and its spiritual decline: "Religion begat prosperity and the daughter devoured the mother."[2] Perhaps this is why Jesus said, "Take care, and be on your guard," when it comes to your possessions (Luke 12:15 ESV).

If you can't take it with you when you go, then now is the time to learn to be generous. Be generous because it is the nature of God to be generous. Think of His generosity to you in Christ. Occasionally I think of the cross as a giant plus sign that reminds me of God's generosity. He became poor so that we, through His poverty, might become rich (2 Corinthians 8:9)!

I (George) often recall my Scottish mother telling me as a boy, in her lilting brogue, "Son, seldom repress a generous impulse." She tried to encourage a generous spirit in her children because of the generous attitude of the Lord.

There is joy that comes in giving. Perhaps this is the greatest reason of all for being generous.

When we stop grasping and give our stuff away, we discover the only true and lasting joy there is—the joy of knowing Christ Himself. We discover that He is enough.

That conversation that I (Don) had with Dr. Nicole had an

interesting ending. Yes, he spoke of his own retrenchment, not with deep complaint but with a proper sense of realism and lament that comes from any loss. There was melancholy in his voice as he reminisced about days gone by and noted what he no longer had.

But then he paused in the conversation. And with all the vigor of his French-accented English, he emphatically exclaimed, "But I have joy." And this, he said, could not be taken away! Not only that, but Dr. Nicole clearly understood that his period of retrenchment is a season that would soon be over.

We ended the visit by opening up the Scriptures and reading together from Psalm 16. That great psalm begins, "Keep me safe, O God, for in you I take refuge. I said to the Lord, 'You are my Lord; apart from you I have no good thing.' . . .You have assigned me my portion and my cup . . . Therefore my heart is glad and my tongue rejoices."

With particular eagerness, Dr. Nicole recited from memory as I read the last part of the psalm. "My body also will rest secure, because you will not abandon me to the grave, nor will you let your Holy One see decay. You have made known to me the path of life; you will fill me with joy in your presence, with eternal pleasures at your right hand" (Psalm 16:9–11).

Seeing beyond our seasons of accumulation and retrenchment, Dr. Nicole reveled in a deeper joy. He clearly had his eye on another season, which for him was just around the corner.

9

DEALING WITH SUFFERING

And Making a Tiny Bit of Sense of It

"WHEN I LAY THESE QUESTIONS BEFORE
GOD I GET NO ANSWER. BUT A RATHER
SPECIAL SORT OF 'NO ANSWER.'"

"IT IS NOT THE LOCKED DOOR. IT IS MORE LIKE A
SILENT, CERTAINLY NOT UNCOMPASSIONATE,
GAZE. AS THOUGH HE SHOOK HIS HEAD NOT
IN REFUSAL BUT WAIVING THE QUESTION. LIKE,
'PEACE, CHILD; YOU DON'T UNDERSTAND.'"
—C. S. LEWIS, *A GRIEF OBSERVED*

LIVE LONG ENOUGH and you will suffer. Some suffer early in life; many suffer late in life. To complicate matters, living longer means suffering more. When the psalmist said, "The length of our days is seventy years—or eighty, if we have the strength," he added, "yet their span is but trouble and sorrow" (Psalm 90:10).

Those who have lived long have seen it all. They have experienced many mountains and many valleys, many victories and a whole lot of defeats. They've known disappointment. They've probably known sickness. They have tasted tragedy. In some ways, it is hard to have a naïve faith when you live as many decades as I have. Not only have you suffered, but you have had time to test your beliefs and think things through.

I (George) had my first big taste of trouble when I was a twenty-year-old student at Moody Bible Institute in 1944. All of a sudden, I was experiencing pains where I should not be experiencing them. I went to see my doctor at Chicago's Swedish Covenant Hospital. I told him I had what felt like a toothache in my groin. Dr. Titus Johnson put me through a series of tests, and sure enough, after taking a biopsy, he discovered I had a tumor in my testicle. It was quite large and worse, it was malignant. That's not the kind of news a college student wants to hear.

Dr. Johnson said I would need several surgeries. I also underwent thirty rough, nausea-inducing radiation treatments (it was primitive back then!). That's when he told me I might not survive this cancer, and if I did, I would probably not be able to have children. I had no idea what was happening to my life. But by God's grace, it all went better than any of us expected.

Of course, my troubles did not end there. I had another bout with cancer in my late 50s while I was president of Moody. This time, it was prostate cancer. I had to do more rounds of radiation treatments, all of which did a number on my bladder.

In between those two experiences, we've had many joys but also sorrows. My wife and I have had four children whom we love. But we've also had the heartache of children who have strayed from the Lord. We've experienced the joys of daughters-in-law, grandchildren, and even great-grandchildren. But we've also experienced several divorces with all their emotional, life-draining turmoil.

As a pastor, each church was a blessing and a challenge. We

saw people come to faith in Christ and families healed. But we had disappointments with people, including disappointment with myself.

While working for a parachurch ministry, it was much the same. Many extraordinary privileges came with the job. But I've had to make difficult decisions that were misunderstood, and I experienced all the flak that comes with being a change agent. I've had board members try to oust me and staff members undermine me. With each of these experiences came sleepless nights.

The most painful experience our family ever had came when my high school-aged granddaughter died of a drug overdose. It was so unexpected. We were so close. It was a devastating blow to our whole family.

And these days, while I am glad to still be serving in ministry, my body does not always cooperate with me—whether it's side effects from all that radiation or sciatic nerves that shoot pain through my body.

Through these experiences I have often asked, "Lord why?" or "Lord, how long?"

Still, I've not really experienced the kind of suffering that so many people in the world experience. I've never experienced extreme poverty or hunger. I have not had to face brute injustice and oppression. Nor have I been physically persecuted for my faith, like the many martyrs, including some of my friends who have died for Christ.

Nevertheless, I have had seasons of affliction, and sometimes I simply could not make sense of it.

THERE IS MUCH WE DO
NOT KNOW ABOUT SUFFERING

Why did some of these things happen to me and not others? Why does it come at the time of life when it does? Why does it come in the prime of youth for some, but not for another? Why do some who are young suffer so much? Why are some episodes of suffering so incredibly hard? For that matter, why do troubles seem to come in waves? And why do some people seem to get a whole lot more of it than others? These are real questions, and they often go unanswered.

I've noticed in Scripture that many people faced the mystery of suffering. Think of Job. His friends thought they knew why he was afflicted, but they were misinformed. In the end, even Job did not know the answer to his own dark night of the soul.

When my granddaughter unexpectedly died, we received many phone calls from people who tried to console us. People were trying to be helpful. But sometimes the things they said didn't help—like asking if we'd gotten over it yet! As though you can ever "get over" losing a child or a grandchild.

Think of the book of Ruth. That story begins with three widows whose husbands died early. They did not know why. Naomi's opinion was simply that "the Almighty has made my life very bitter. I went away full, but the Lord has brought me back empty" (Ruth 1:20–21).

Mary and Martha did not know why their brother, Lazarus, died, until they were with Jesus. Before then, their grief was great, and they were full of questions. *Why?* they wondered. "Lord, if you had been here," they said. In other words, "Lord, why weren't you here?" (see John 11:21).

The psalmist, in Psalm 88, was full of questions for his suffering. He was tossed in a dark pit and abandoned. His body was captive and his soul was full of trouble. Some scholars think this is the psalm Jesus had on His lips when He was held in the basement of Caiaphas the high priest's house. Archaeologists have found a large empty cistern underneath the house that may have been used as a prison where Jesus spent part of that night. There was no escape, so He cried out for help, asking, "Why, O Lord, do you reject me and hide your face from me?" (v. 14). Certainly Jesus' question from the cross underscores my point. In that dark hour He cried, "My God, my God, why have you forsaken me?" (Matthew 27:46).

In our seasons of suffering, we also ask the "why" question. We are looking for the grand answer, though it may not be readily apparent. Besides, Scripture gives many possible reasons for suffering. Which might be the explanation for my suffering? And is it wise to even look for one reason? Are there overlapping reasons that explain what we are going through?

Possible reasons for suffering include a range of things—living in a fallen world (Romans 8:22), natural consequences for wrongdoing (Romans 1:27; Galatians 6:7), God's direct judgment for wrongdoing (Genesis 6:5ff; Acts 12:20–23; 1 Corinthians 11:28–30), God's fatherly discipline (Proverbs 3:11–12; Hebrews 12:4–11), the consequences of another's sin (Genesis 37–50; 2 Samuel 11; Psalm 42–43), the cost of following Christ (John 15:18–20; Philippians 3:10; 2 Timothy 3:12), satanic opposition (Ephesians 6:10–12; Job 1–2), the price of sacrificing for others (2 Corinthians 1:3–7), our own maturity and growth in Christ (Romans 5:3–5; James 1:3–4), structural injustice (Luke 18:2), to prepare us for heaven (2 Corinthians 4:17), and to display the power, glory, and purposes of God (Genesis 37–50; John 9:11ff; 2 Corinthians 12.9). There are many possible reasons for suffering.

Then there are the deeper questions that face us. There is the origin of evil. Why was it allowed in the first place? How does God allow it, yet stand against it? Even theologians must admit partial ignorance to these deep questions. We do not have the full explanation.

For that matter, there is the question of God's goodness. Why have we in the West experienced so much of His mercy—to the extent that it makes seasons of suffering seem like an aberration? Christian believers in the Islamic world and in the developing world view things much differently.

Along with that there comes the question of how suffering fits within God's providence. How can He be sovereign over it and yet still hold us accountable for our own evil? This question too remains a mystery.

If you haven't noticed, asking God tough questions is very biblical. Godly lament and complaint, which is often included in the Psalms, is acceptable if it comes from a respectful heart. It's okay to articulate our confusion and honest struggles to God in prayer.

I've titled this chapter "Dealing with Suffering and Making a Tiny Bit of Sense Out of It" because there is much that does not seem to make sense when we suffer.

When C. S. Lewis wrestled with his wife, Joy's, death, he filled several notebooks with questions and complaints to God. He struggled with the fact of divine sovereignty and human suffering. Lewis wrote:

When I lay these questions before God I get no answer. But a rather special sort of "No answer." It is not the locked door. It is more like a silent, certainly not uncompassionate, gaze. As though He shook His head not in refusal but waiving the question. Like, "Peace, child; you don't understand."[1]

SOME THINGS WE DO
KNOW ABOUT SUFFERING

While we all have many unanswered questions about our own suffering, we are not left totally in the dark. Unlike Job, Ruth, and Naomi, we have more resources at our disposal to make some sense of what happens to us. Though we too "see but a poor reflection as in a mirror," as Paul put it in 1 Corinthians 13:12, we have more clarity than these Old Testament saints because we have the wisdom and insight of two biblical testaments. Together they give us resources to process and endure in our pain and suffering. Let me explain.

First, we have the revelation of a God who stands over suffering yet who has entered into it. He is the sovereign Lord. To say God is sovereign means that He reigns. He reigns over this universe. According to the Bible, He truly does have "the whole world in His hands." Nothing is outside of His sovereignty—or He is not sovereign.

All this means that He allows what happens to us for His purposes. We do not always know those purposes. But at such times we submit to His wisdom and pray, "Lord, I know that You know what You're doing, even though I don't know what You're doing." Sometimes I know of no other response than to cry out, "Oh, the depth of the riches and wisdom and knowledge of God! How unsearchable are his judgments and how inscrutable his ways! For who has known the mind of the Lord? . . ." (Romans 11:33–34 ESV).

And yet, the sovereign God revealed in Scripture is a sovereign who suffers. By His incarnation we see that He cares so much for this world that He chose to enter it and become human. He suffered loss. He became acquainted with grief. He bore our sorrows on the cross.

Sometimes people ask, "Where was God when this evil event happened?" The biblical reply is that He is right where He was when He sent His Son into this broken world on that first Christmas day, and right where He was when His Son bore the sins of the world on that Good Friday. That is where He is. That is the kind of God He is. Not distant but near. Both things are true about Him. He is sovereign but a suffering sovereign. This brings great comfort to those who experience affliction.

Second, we have a credible story that helps us process our suffering. The story line of the Bible gives us a framework to process the hard things that come into our lives. It is the story of creation, fall, redemption, and consummation. It is not an exhaustive explanation, but it is comprehensive.

That story begins with creation—that God made this world for His glory and our pleasure, and He created it good! But then the story continues with the fall. Humanity rebelled against God. This disobedience brought tragic consequences. Evil and injustice were unleashed. Sin and death took root—and pervade this world as a fracturing force. Reverberations of brokenness are seen everywhere and in everyone. We live life under the curse.

I sometimes hear about pastors who lose their faith and say

they cannot believe in a God who allows injustice and suffering. When I hear this, I wonder which Bible have they been reading? Which gospel have they been proclaiming? If anyone, Christians (let alone pastors) should not be surprised by suffering. It is not only part of living outside of Eden, it is also an inherent part of our story. Of all people, we should be realistic about the world's current condition and its need of a Savior.

Third, we have a Savior who powerfully addresses the problem of suffering through His cross and resurrection. The Bible story line continues with the gospel. After the fall comes the theme of redemption. "God was reconciling the world to himself in Christ" (2 Corinthians 5:19). The problem of sin, death, and evil is answered through the life, death, and resurrection of Christ. God will stamp them out without destroying those who are in Christ. That is why the grand theme of the Bible is "salvation through faith in Christ Jesus" (2 Timothy 3.15).

A fourth resource we have to process the pains of life is this: we have a future that reverses suffering! We are people of hope because the end of the Bible's story line is consummation. Christ will come again to defeat His enemies, judge the nations, reign in this world, and create a new heaven and earth. This is the story's climax, the last word. The Bible moves from paradise, to paradise lost, to paradise regained in Christ.

Fifth, we have ample evidence that our suffering can be redemptive. Without erasing all the mysteries and unanswered questions, because of what God has done in Christ on the cross, because of the numerous examples in the Bible, we know that "for those who love God all things work together for good" (Romans 8:28 ESV). Or as you sometimes hear Christians say, "Life is hard, but God is good!"

That is my story. My cancer bed became a turning point in my life. For believers, the place of suffering often becomes the place where God chastens, fashions character, and renews. As C. H. Spurgeon once put it, "I am certain that I never did grow in grace onehalf so much anywhere as I have upon the bed of pain."[2]

These are the resources that help us process our suffering. We have the revelation of a God who stands over suffering yet has entered into it. We have the credible story line of the Bible that helps us process our suffering. We have a Savior who powerfully addresses the problem of suffering through His cross and resurrection. We have a future that reverses suffering. And we have ample evidence that our suffering can be redemptive.

These resources not only help us process our pains, but they also enable us to live courageously in spite of our suffering.

Don't let your affliction be your excuse to exempt yourself from Christian service or to drop out of the race.

Some of the most extraordinary Christians have made their contribution in the midst of suffering—not easily but faithfully and through the Lord's strength.

Corrie Ten Boom is a great example of a second-halfer who lived well into her 80s. She suffered horrendously under the hands of the Nazis. She experienced great loss. She lost her possessions, her home, and family members. In her book *The Hiding Place*, she explains how after being released from the concentration camp at the end of World War II, she was almost ready to give up. But she was transformed by Christ's love to put away bitterness and love her enemies. The Lord's love propelled her, as an old woman, to travel around the world and tell her story. She worked and taught in sixty-one countries on both sides of the Iron Curtain. To whomever she spoke—African students on the shores of Lake Victoria, farmers in a Cuban sugar field, prisoners in an English penitentiary, or factory workers in Uzbekistan—she brought the truth of the gospel learned in Ravensbruck that "Jesus can turn any loss into glory."

Joni Eareckson Tada has lived with a disability most of her life. Her suffering dates from an accident she had at age 17 when she dived into the Chesapeake Bay during a family outing and crashed into a sandbar, severing her spinal cord. Not only was she almost completely paralyzed, ever since she has never had a day without pain. But through it all she has ministered to both disabled and able-bodied people around the world through books, radio, and conference speaking. She would say that the Lord has been magnified through her weakness.

Charles Spurgeon, a nineteenth-century megachurch pastor in London, produced a massive amount of sermon material that is still read and published. Yet Spurgeon, who died in his 50s, struggled with depression for many years. He once told his students, "The strong are not always vigorous."[3] He was living proof.

And then there is the extraordinary example of John Calvin—one of the most influential Bible teachers of all time. Calvin suffered from poor digestion, migraines, kidney stones, gout, lung infections, and hemorrhages. Once he was gravely ill and a friend found him sitting in bed writing a letter.

"You need to rest. Put away your work," said the friend.

"What?!" Calvin exclaimed. "Would you have the Lord find me idle when he comes?"[4]

All these individuals had good reason to give up and stop serving. Suffering—and the mystery of suffering—can easily become an excuse to immobilize us. The "why" question (Lord, why is this happening to me?) can intellectually paralyze us. Until, that is, we refocus and turn from the "why" to the "what" question and ask, "Lord, what do You want me to do?" That is a question that can more easily be answered.

When we switch questions, that is often a transforming moment. New doors of opportunity open, and His strength is made perfect in our weakness (2 Corinthians 12:9).

10

REVISE YOUR BUCKET LIST

Getting Your Relational House in Order

"GOING AROUND THE WORLD, SEEING EVEREST
OR PARACHUTING OUT OF A PLANE IS GREAT,
BUT IT ISN'T SOMETHING WE NECESSARILY HAVE
TO DO TO BE FULFILLED . . . THE MOST IMPORTANT
THINGS IN LIFE ARE YOUR RELATIONSHIPS."
—ROB REINER, DIRECTOR OF *THE BUCKET LIST*

EDWARD COLE AND Carter Chambers were both diagnosed with cancer and given a year or less to live. Cole was a wealthy hospital magnate—a high achiever, but with a string of dysfunctional family relationships. Carter was a blue-collar auto mechanic and family man. These two men couldn't be more different, yet they were thrown into the same hospital room sharing the same prognosis. Now they both had to come to terms with who they were and how they would make the most of their remaining days. That is the story line for the 2007 film *The Bucket List.*

It was Chambers's little scribbled list that captured Cole's imagination. Chambers, played by Morgan Freeman, said, "The bucket list is a list of things you want to do before you kick the bucket."

The movie struck a chord with older theatergoers. It's a story about running out of time and coming up with our own list as we think through the last chapter of our lives.

What would you like to do before you "kick the bucket"?

Cole, played by Jack Nicholson, wants to drink life to the last drop. So he writes his own list and invites the mechanic Chambers into a rich man's adventure. Cole takes him on a journey of firsts. So they leave the hospital room and for the first time go skydiving. Next, they race each other in classic cars on a professional track. Then they take a private jet around the world to see the pyramids, observe Everest, ride motorcycles on the Great Wall of China, and go to the North Pole.

At the end of the film, the billion-dollar businessman has lots of money, and now lots of amazing adventures, but still has very few good relationships. So, because of meeting Carter Chambers, he starts to reassess everything.

The film makes two key points. First, it's not enough to react to life on a day-to-day basis. People need a road map—life lists that help them set priorities and navigate. But the film's other main point is that good relationships should be very high on every person's bucket list. Flying an airplane, climbing a mountain, learning Mandarin, driving on the Autobahn, owning a beach house, winning an international competition, visiting the Holy Land, riding in a hot air balloon, and whatever else is on your list are simply not enough.

Do you have a bucket list? Do you have an agenda for the remaining years of your life?

Both of us have always been big on goals. We are doers and listmakers. We have told our children things like this: "It's important to have goals! If you aim at nothing, you will hit it every time! Make goals early, review them regularly, and post them on your bathroom mirror so you look at them every day! Goals are magic; they streamline your mind and energies! Set goals for the different areas of your life—spiritual goals, physical goals, career goals, hobby goals, etc.!"

Our children have often rolled their eyes when they've listened to us both repeat these "doer" platitudes.

One of the perennial flaws of task-oriented people is that we so focus on our task that we overlook key relationships. We are more like Edward Cole than we want to admit. We are so locked into "doing" that we forget to think about "being."

We admit that we've been slow to realize the importance of key relationships. Yet the longer we live, and the more we study the Bible and theology, the more convinced we become that we have made a big mistake and that relationships really, really matter.

But even this does not put it strongly enough. Relationships matter because at the heart of reality is a Holy Trinity—a relational being of perfect love—the triune God. By gazing on the beauty of God, we not only come to see how important relationships are, but we see a perfect relationship, a blessed community, and we find our own vision for loving others strengthened.

Simply put, if we ignore relationships, we are out of sync with reality. If we enter into the second half of life with our own agendas in hand but have no time for the key relationships of our lives, we are missing it!

We'd like to urge you to revise your bucket list.

One of the most important things you must do in the second half of life is to get your relational house in order. Many of us know what it means to get our financial house in order. So we meet with a financial advisor to discuss our estate plan—pensions, life insurance policies, investments, etc. Some businesses will draft business succession plans and take out what they call "key-man insurance" so the firm can carry on if it loses a vital staff member. We know what it means to get our legal house in order. That's why we go to a lawyer and make a will.

But what about our relationships? More particularly, what do we do about the broken relationships?

THE WORST FUNERALS
WE HAVE EVER ATTENDED

In the next chapter we write about some of the best funerals we've ever attended. But before we get there, we'd like to take a few minutes and share with you some of the worst ones we've attended.

I (George) will never forget the funeral of a man I will call Sam. This guy was a hard-drinking, rugged truck driver who could not say a sentence without a string of creative profanity coming out of his mouth! Yet Sam came to Christ at a Word of Life rally at Yankee Stadium. Talk about a radical conversion! Everything began to change. Sam and I became close friends. I helped disciple him in his new faith.

Sam's family was not happy about his change of lifestyle. They preferred the old Sam. His wife and children turned against him and booted him out. His friends said they liked it better when Sam would drink and party with them. There were lots of broken relationships.

Suddenly, at a Memorial Day picnic while playing volleyball, Sam dropped dead at age 55. Jack Wyrtzen, Hermann Braunlin, and I officiated at the funeral. Everyone showed up, I mean everyone. The funeral home was jammed. Sam had a gospel tract written about how he used to be and how Christ changed his life. This tract was available at the funeral parlor.

Sam's son, another hard-drinking truck driver, did not like it when during the service Pastor Braunlin read a section of this tract describing Sam's old life. The son had been drinking, so he stood up in the middle of the funeral service and shouted, "One more word out of you, and you will be laying in the casket with my father!"

People gasped. Some cried. Herrmann went speechless! Clearly shaken, he wasn't sure what to do.

So I stood up abruptly and said, "Let us pray." And I did. I prayed a long prayer as two of my large, burly, truck-driving deacons moved to either side of the half-drunken son. The service was short, and there was no more trouble out of this guy.

Every pastor knows that the two family occasions that spark the most tension are weddings and funerals.

This might sound strange, but think about it. Weddings and especially funerals are the two emotional moments when family dynamics most come to the surface. At a funeral, if family relationships are bad, the added elements of grief and regret greatly increase the potential for blowups. Throw into the mix the issue of children fighting over inheritance money, and it gets even worse.

We've had people bring guns to funerals, had fights erupt outside, and have been warned not to say this or that or a family member might come after us. Countless times we've both felt the ice of broken or strained relationships.

Sometimes family members who have not talked to each other

for years decide to show up for the funeral. Memories of the past flood their minds. For years the acid of bitterness and unforgiveness has eaten away at their souls. Often such people wish to set the story straight, to dredge up the conflict yet again, and pick up where the last fight left off. It's ugly. These are the dynamics of the worst funerals we've ever attended!

But for a disciple of Jesus, there has to be a better way. And there is. God's Word calls us to "be patient, bearing with one another in love," and to "make every effort to keep the unity of the Spirit through the bond of peace" (Ephesians 4:1–3). Rather than be people who "harbor bitter envy," we are told that "the wisdom that comes from heaven is first of all pure, then peace-loving, considerate, submissive, full of mercy and good fruit, impartial and sincere. Peacemakers who sow in peace raise a harvest of righteousness" (James 3:17–18).

If you head out on this path, you will begin to set your relational house in order. In fact, we are told in Matthew 5:24 that if we are going to worship and in the process of offering our gift, remember that our brother there has something against us, we are to stop.

"Leave your gift there before the altar and go," Jesus said. "First be reconciled to your brother, and then come and offer your gift" (ESV).

Now here is a familiar setting. Two people are at church and they are angry with each other. But they are still going to meet with God and want to ignore the broken relationship. Jesus says, "Don't!" He says, "Stop." He calls us to keep short accounts with each other, to not let these things fester. Instead He calls us to do whatever is necessary to restore harmony. After that we can come back and offer our gift. He wants the worshiper to get his or her priorities right!

There is a message here for second-halfers! We do not know how many years we have left. As we ready ourselves to be with the Lord, we are called to drop what we are doing and get our relational house in order.

So first revise your bucket list. If there are key relationships that are broken, put this at the top of your list. Do the things that make for peace. You will never regret it.

Next, take inventory. What relationships in your life need completing or mending? We second-halfers are old enough to have left relational trails. What kind of trail have you left?

How are things with your children? What about colleagues and people at church? Enter a season of prayer and ask the Spirit of God to convict you about what you should address. Along with this, ask for input from your spouse, your small group, your pastor, or colleagues. Tell them you are revising your bucket list and that this is one of your priorities. Tell them you need their help.

We are not looking for a catalog of everyone you've ever slighted or disappointed. What we are after is a list of those people you have clearly wronged. As you pray, you will know this in your spirit, and which broken relationships grieve the Holy Spirit.

Once God reveals to you those relationships that need attention, do some introspection. First, ask how you can honor the Lord in these relationships. Bring the conflict before Him. Ask what would please Him. What would He have you do? He might whisper to you to stop pretending the conflict does not exist. He might convict you to stop the trash-talking about these people.

Second, do a spiritual MRI on your heart and see where you

have contributed to the broken relationship. Forget, if you can, what the other person did to wrong you. You cannot control them or their reactions. Focus exclusively on what you have done to wrong them. In the words of Matthew 7:5, examine the plank in your own eye. Take responsibility for your own contributions to the breakdown. Focus on what you can control.

And third, ask the Lord to show you how you can demonstrate forgiveness and encourage a reasonable solution to this conflict. What will it take to make things right? This will prove the genuineness of your motives to the person you want to meet with.

Only after taking these steps are you prepared to reach out to the person. But you must do this. Make the first move and stop waiting for them to come to you. Realize they will probably be suspicious of your approach. They may not even receive it. No matter. Try to set up a meeting in the most nonthreatening place and in the most nonthreatening way possible.

At this point, you are ready to say what you need to say. Remember, don't focus on what they did wrong. Focus on what you did wrong. You can tell them that God has been convicting you about this. You can even tell them you were hurt by what happened.

This is when you sincerely apologize. We don't mean an "I'm sorry you felt bad" or "I'm sorry you were hurt" kind of apology. That is no apology at all. We are talking about the kind where you clearly take responsibility for what you did wrong and say, "I am sorry for my part. I was wrong. Please forgive me."

Here you must think clearly about the grace of forgiveness. If you are "in Christ," God has provided you a great and generous forgiveness. You are depending on this when you get to heaven. Keep in mind the words of the Lord's Prayer, which says, "forgive us our debts, as we also have forgiven our debtors" (Matthew 6:12). Out of God's forgiveness to us should flow gratitude that moves us to forgive others. That is why Paul says, "Be kind and compassionate to one another, forgiving each other, just as in Christ God forgave you" (Ephesians 4:32).

It is impossible to predict the other person's response. This is not under your control. All you can do is be obedient and do the right thing.

But you can pray that this encounter will lead to reconciliation. The more generous your response to the offended person, the more likely reconciliation will be. After tax collector Zacchaeus began to follow Jesus, he was convicted that he had cheated people. The proof of his faith was returning the money—fourfold—to those he had cheated (Luke 19:1–8). If you have hurt someone deeply, remember that trust is not rebuilt in a day. For reconciliation to take place requires real evidence of change. If the damage was really deep, repairing the relationship will take a lot of proof and a lot of time. That's what made Zacchaeus's turnaround so genuine. People knew he meant business.

BEYOND PEACE TO BLESSING

When it comes to those close to us, peace in the relationship should not be our final goal. If God grants this peace, it is a wonderful thing. But then move beyond peace to blessing. Actively work to bless this person. Show them your love. Tell them you love them. Prove it to them.

We've both heard too many stories of parents who did not verbalize their love to their children. We've both met too many wounded children who longed to hear those words but never did!

So while you have opportunity, with the remaining days God gives you, seek to be a blessing to those people. The best way to get your relational house in order comes when you move all the way from cursing to actively blessing another person. You leave them a legacy of blessing rather than one of pain and disappointment.

WHAT WILL LAST?

A few years ago, I (Don) had a humbling experience. I was in Scotland looking for the graves of my ancestors. Wouldn't it be neat, I thought, if I could find their gravestones—these remaining memorials to their lives? Well, I did find their graves. But what shocked me is that the cemetery was in disrepair. The stones were broken. The inscriptions were fading. And no one was caring for the upkeep. No one had visited these places in a long, long time. The memorials were almost gone.

That was a humbling moment. I thought, What lasts? What in our lives really lasts?

Our things won't last. They will be dispersed to others or tossed in one of those large driveway trash bins. My library won't last. The only people whose libraries last are US presidents. So forget about that one. And now I see that our gravestones won't last long. Time will wear the inscription away, or vandals will destroy it. The only things that will last are your relationships with God and with others. Love lasts.

First Corinthians 13 tells us that many things will pass away— prophecies, tongues, knowledge, possessions. But then it says that "love never fails" (v. 8). As Paul puts it, "And now these three remain: faith, hope and love. But the greatest of these is love" (1 Corinthians 13:13).

Love lasts. This is one of life's greatest lessons. This is why it is so important for people in the second half of life to take steps to not go to the grave with relational regrets, long-standing accounts, and unfinished business. This is why it is so important to revise your bucket list and get your relational house in order.

11

THE BEST FUNERALS WE HAVE EVER ATTENDED

"A GREAT MAN IS ONE SENTENCE."
—Clare Boothe Luce

IN 1962, Clare Boothe Luce had a memorable conversation with President John F. Kennedy. Luce was one of the first women to serve in the US Congress. She was also a journalist, an ambassador, and a playwright. She offered this advice to Kennedy because she feared that the president's attention was so splintered among different priorities. So she said to him, "A great man is one sentence."

Think of it. Abraham Lincoln's sentence was, "He preserved the union and freed the slaves."

Franklin Roosevelt's was, "He led us out of a great depression and helped win World War II."

Reagan's was, "He won the Cold War." Rosa Parks's was, "She kept her seat on the bus and sparked a movement." George W. Bush's was, "He engaged America in the war on terror."

Luce was worried that Kennedy's attention was so unfocused, his sentence "risked becoming a muddled paragraph."[1]

One way to bring greater focus to your life is to think about your sentence. It's true. People will probably summarize our lives in one sentence. Think of it as your "life sentence"! So . . . what do you want your sentence to read—that one sentence you would like people to say about you when your life is over.

Is that thought too much for you? Can't do it in a sentence? Then try this exercise. Let's take a trip. Fast-forward and visit your own funeral.

VISITING YOUR OWN FUNERAL

Friends, family, and coworkers are gathering. Who do you think will show up? As they approach the church, a lone piper is playing. Upon entering quietly, friends and family sign the guest book. They are still somewhat in shock that you are gone. Before the service begins, there is an open-casket viewing. The pastor has already met with the family. As each person approaches your casket, what are they saying? What is their demeanor?

As the service begins, a eulogy is spoken. More than one sentence, a eulogy is like a short speech. The term comes from the Greek word *eulogia*, which means "good words." It's a speech or an essay that praises someone who just died. So what is being said about you? They are summing you up.

Writer and publisher Michael Hyatt in a recent blog encouraged his readers to write their own eulogies. He presented it as an exercise to help us confront our mortality and our legacy. But it can be more than that. It can be an opportunity for us to think with our end in view, for us to think deeply about what we want our legacy to be—and then to aim for it.[2]

He's on to something. This little exercise can help us live each day with greater purpose.

Try it. Go to a cemetery. Visit the grave of a friend and take some extra time for yourself to think, not about what they may say but what you want them to say. Go ahead. Confront your own mortality. Visit your own death. Describe it on one page.

We've told you about the worst funeral we've ever attended. There were more. The bad ones were usually funerals where relationships were in terrible shape. Or else they were the funerals of young children who died early, teenagers killed in automobile accidents, family members killed by domestic violence, or suicides.

But let's shift gears and consider the best funerals we have ever attended. Not that we love funerals. It's just that, as pastors, we have attended many funerals, and some funerals are . . . well . . . better than others.

By and large, the best ones are for senior saints who have lived out a long-distance Christianity. When they die, the gospel is as prominent in their service as it was in their lives. Not only that, but they also leave an amazing legacy—and all the glory seems to go to God. In that respect we agree with the psalmist who wrote, "Precious in the sight of the Lord is the death of his saints" (Psalm 116:15).

STRANGE DAYS IN
THE FUNERAL BUSINESS

As our nation drifts further from its Christian heritage, funerals are getting bizarre. A host of strange new funeral practices are popping up. People are requesting their own music and media that have nothing to do with faith. Some funeral companies now offer fantasy funerals. Choose a theme—rodeo, gaming, fishing, golf, or football. Some companies will make the funeral resemble a party. They also offer designer caskets.

You've no doubt heard of all the unique places where people want their loved one's ashes sprinkled. Forget the cemetery or the columbarium. Besides the home garden, the golf course, the favorite fishing hole or ski run, the most popular places to have ashes scattered are the Grand Canyon, a favorite beach, and Hawaii. Police have found sports fans scattering ashes at the corners of Wrigley Field, Fenway Park, and Yankee Stadium! More cremated remains are surreptitiously spread at Disneyland than any other theme park.[3]

Now, if you're willing to pay the price, you can even have your loved one's cremated remains compressed into a diamond that you can wear as jewelry. If that is not your style, you can get their DNA spliced into a tree, or have their remains freeze-dried, or their ashes mixed with gunpowder and made into fireworks so your loved ones go out with a bang. (We're not making this up!)

This is a far cry from the days when I (George) was growing up. Up until the 1950s, mourning was more public, visitation of the body would often take place at your home, services were held in the church, and burial was not far outside of town—often near or next to the church.

That was then. Today, funeral homes have adopted most of the work of the church. Death and mourning are entirely removed from the home. Sometimes people dispense with services altogether.

Why have a funeral service? There are lots of good reasons.

For one, it offers closure to those who grieve. There is a finality about death that the funeral service seals. Second, a service allows loved ones and community to gather to celebrate and give thanks to God for a person's life. But also, a service brings aid to the grieving by surrounding them with friends and faith.

So what can we say about the best funerals? What are characteristics of good ones? Here are a few that we've observed.

CHARACTERISTICS OF THE BEST FUNERALS

First, they were understandable and faith-building. They were understandable to seasoned churchgoers, unchurched visitors, and even to children who were encouraged to attend. In many funeral services we've attended, the pastor seems to forget that today the average layperson knows little about the Bible. So the person leading it needs to be warm, personable, and clear.

These services remind you about what is important. They help us measure our lives by the lives of others. They help us "number our days."

These days many parents often shield children from funerals in the name of protecting them. Yet a funeral gives them a sense of reality and helps them think about their own mortality.

A good funeral teaches lessons from the life of the deceased. It highlights good qualities. True, at some funerals they over-eulogize. It's always tempting for those who get up and speak to do this. Nevertheless, a great funeral takes a life that has been well lived (a life that exemplified the great truths and virtues of the Bible) and gently yet clearly sets forth what is important to admonish those listening.

Second, a great funeral will offer worship to God. It will focus not only on comforting the bereaved but also on praising God for being God. No matter what the circumstances of the death, a great funeral will recognize that every day we have is a gift, and we have no right to even one.

People therefore will thank God for His goodness in the life of the newly departed. They will worship God because of His sovereignty and love. They will sing hymns of praise to God—along the lines of "How Great Thou Art" or "How Great Is Our God."

Third, a great funeral will be Christ-centered and gospel-centered. That's ultimately what makes a Christian funeral different. Because it is shaped by Christ's death and resurrection, it abounds in hope.

Many memorial services these days seem to put all the emphasis on the life of the deceased.

 The focus has shifted from a proper eulogy and thanksgiving, to almost an exclusive focus on the person who died—with little emphasis on the God who gives life, takes away life, and gives eternal life through Jesus Christ.

We see this most clearly when comparing how much time is given in a funeral service to speaking about the person—or about God. We've both been in many churches where God does not get to speak, because His Word is hardly read at all. Such services are more of a sentimental memory fest with a little Bible thrown in at the end. After the "open mic" time, where people share memories, everyone is too spent to listen to the Scriptures or hear the Word preached. There has been a shift in emphasis away from God, the

Bible, and the great truths of the Christian faith that sustain us in the face of death.

While still including open sharing or eulogizing, great funerals shift the balance back to where God's Word and the gospel get the primary place—where Christ's cross and resurrection become the lenses through which we interpret this loss.

In the best funerals a pastor is able to affirm the faith of the deceased person and rejoice in the hope of heaven. But sometimes a pastor does not have sufficient reason to affirm the faith of the deceased. In that instance all he can do is simply affirm *the* faith—and point people to the only One who can save us from the second death.

You've no doubt heard about the woman whose last wish was to be laid in a casket with a fork in her hand. She was not heavy, so the symbolism had nothing to do with a love of eating. Rather it was her way of announcing hope to all who passed by her casket. She held that fork in anticipation of sitting with Christ and His people at the great and future marriage supper of the Lamb. It was quite different from those funerals where there is no hope—only loss, tragedy, grief, despair, and finality in the face of death.

Fourth, the best funerals we've attended have been well prepared. Not just by the church but well prepared by the deceased before they died. They gave some time to thinking about their funeral before it happened. They made a plan. Your pastor will gladly help you come up with a plan if you don't yet have one.

Death is often a stressful event for friends and family. It affects them spiritually, emotionally, and physically. People are so frazzled, they often do not think straight. So a little preparation helps everyone.

Planning for great funerals usually begins with the resolve to honor the Lord in the funeral service. That resolution will affect everything else that takes place.

Planning includes gathering key information for the family ahead of time. This would include financial information, a will, and a list of important relationships and contacts. It also would include significant information on your life, so that when an obituary is written, there is a basic life summary with key dates, places you have lived, jobs you've held, etc.

Planning should also include working out issues such as the following: What kind of service would you like—a funeral (where the body is present and usually followed by a private graveside service) or a memorial (where the body is not present, often held after the graveside service)? Will you be donating organs? Where will your remains lie? Will there be a burial or a cremation? Where will the service be? Who will officiate? Where will memorial gifts go? What will be the Scripture readings and songs? And if there is a casket, who will be the pallbearers?

In our opinion, good planning also includes identifying your favorite Bible verse or passages that your pastor might speak about. I (Don) usually request to see the person's Bible so I get a sense of what Scripture texts captured their attention. You learn a lot from looking at someone's Bible. I will sometimes even preach the funeral sermon from their Bible!

One other great preparation tool is to have a written testimony on file with your pastor. This will not only help your pastor get to know you, but it will also help at the time of death. Then your own words can be read—and you get to have a part in proclaiming the gospel to others. My friend John Haggai has even recorded his own funeral sermon ahead of time! As a former pastor, he decided that, as he said, "Anyone who has my service will probably say stuff that isn't true and say that I am better than I am. So at least now I know what will be said and it will be accurate. It will be honest, straight, and honor God."

We both have friends who have video-recorded their testimony to be played at their funeral—sometimes even containing an appeal to receive Christ as Savior! Coming directly from the deceased person makes the appeal more powerful.

Finally, the best funerals we have ever attended are church-based. They radically counteract the modern idea that death is a solitary event. Instead, the church family plays a primary role.

Death becomes a community moment. We don't have to go through it alone. Instead, we are surrounded by others who share our sorrow.

As the community gathers for a service, together we reacquaint ourselves with the story line of the Bible, which helps us make sense of this death. We proclaim Christ crucified and risen, and that by His great work, death has been defeated.

We also affirm that the departed in Christ is now part of the church triumphant. They are now rejoicing in heaven, while we (what theologians call the "church militant") are still on earth engaged in the work of the gospel and serving as His soldiers.

We affirm the communion of the saints. That even those who die are still members of the body of Christ and still very much alive in the presence of Christ. Or as that old country classic put it, "Will the circle be unbroken? Bye and bye, Lord, bye and bye." The song was written about the death of a godly mother. It looked forward to the reunion of the redeemed.

These then are the characteristics of the best funerals we have ever attended. Such funerals become an opportunity for spiritual formation as we are reshaped by biblical truths in the midst of life's hardships.

Taken together they remind us that a person is really more than a sentence, as Clare Boothe Luce contended. A person is also much more than a eulogy. But thinking about these things ahead of time enables us to influence how that eulogy will sound on the day it is spoken.

The good news is, if you are reading this, today is a day of grace, a day of opportunity. You are still writing your sentence! Perhaps this brief experience of "visiting your death" will inspire you to become more intent on strengthening your legacy . . . and finishing well.

12

WHAT WE HAVE LEARNED ABOUT FINISHING WELL

"IF ONLY I MAY FINISH THE RACE AND COMPLETE THE TASK THE LORD JESUS HAS GIVEN ME—THE TASK OF TESTIFYING TO THE GOSPEL OF GOD'S GRACE."
—Acts 20:24

THE PHRASE "FINISHING WELL" means different things to different people. For some, finishing well means ending life with a long, cushy retirement. For those who believe "he who dies with the most toys wins," finishing well means having lots of stuff. For still others, it means ending with a pain-free death.

When we use the phrase "finishing well," we mean following Christ to the very end of our lives, finishing His assignments for us, and hearing His "well done, good and faithful servant."

Some of us grew up singing the old gospel song, "I Have Decided." Do you know it? The refrain goes: "I have decided to follow Jesus. I have decided to follow Jesus. I have decided to follow Jesus. No turning back, no turning back." It's a song we've probably sung hundreds of times.

But while many start out with great intentions to follow Jesus, some do turn back. They don't finish well. The Bible gives ample testimony of people who ended life poorly. Lot pitched his tent toward Sodom. Then he sat in the gates of that city. His children married outside of their faith and laughed at Lot when he said judgment was coming. Eli the priest ended poorly. He failed to discipline his sons, and this brought great trouble to his family. Saul had such potential. Sadly, at the end of his life we see him consulting a medium for guidance and then taking his own life. Solomon was given the gift of wisdom, but in the end his unbelieving wives caused him to drift from the Lord. These are only a few of the biblical stories of those who did not finish well.

We've seen this played out in our day many times. A dad has a large family, but as the financial pressure mounts, he bolts. A business executive has remarkable success, but it ruins him and his faith falters. A pastor leaves the ministry after revelations of sexual unfaithfulness. A missionary leaves his post after his team encounters the difficulties of living in another culture.

WHY MANY DO NOT FINISH WELL

Why do many not finish well? It's been said that our enemy, the roaring lion, can knock us off course in a hundred ways. Here are a few of them.

Our trouble always begins with **spiritual drift**. Like the Ephesian church, we lose our first love.

Intimacy with God diminishes. We plateau. We take our eyes off Christ. Our hearts then wander. Our own evil desires carry us away, and we get caught up in some spiritual idolatry.

Sometimes the problem is **pride**. After a few successes we start to take credit that is not ours.

We begin to rely on our own strength. We've become self-centered and we don't even know it. We are blind to our own self-sufficiency. Like David in the Bible, our first impulse is to number our people, not to rely on the Lord.

Pride can manifest itself in many ways. It can take the shape of self-absorbed ambition, where we are so intent on gaining a reputation that we make major compromises. It can show itself in the abuse of power. As we rise to the top, we enjoy the accompanying perks. But then something changes, and we develop a sense of entitlement. We assume privileges that are not ours. Too often there is no one to hold us accountable for what we are doing. In the Bible, Saul and Uzziah did this when they tried to take priestly privileges.

Besides pride, **sexual sin** has been the downfall of many leaders. There is first an inward fall.

Overworked or restless or on the road, we begin to view things on the TV or Internet that pollute our souls. Walls of defense start coming down. Then, perhaps when our relationships at home are not well, we get lonely or tired or empty. In an unguarded moment, we flirt with illicit relationships to add spark to our lives. And once Satan makes that first entrance in our lives, once he gets that foothold, it is not easy to get him out. This is what happened to David when he coveted another man's wife.

Busyness has been the downfall of some. We don't take proper care of ourselves. There is no time for silence or solitude. We think everything depends on us, so we keep going hard. But in our busyness, we tank spiritually. Socrates said, "Beware of the barrenness of an over-busy life."

He was on to something.

And if not busyness, what about **greed**? Jesus said, "Be on your guard against all kinds of greed" (Luke 12:15). Did He know something that we've forgotten? Did He know that materialism does something to our spirit? When our lives are filled with so much stuff, we become preoccupied with the cares of this world. Our spirits choke. They have no room to breathe. This too is subtle yet deadly. No one sees it coming. But its effect is devastating spiritually. Greed can involve abuse of finances or plain old domination by the love of money and things. In the Bible, this is what happened to Ananias and Sapphira in the New Testament, and to Gideon (with his golden ephod) in the Old Testament.

Family trouble is yet another way we get derailed and do not finish well. Intense conflict between a husband and wife can destroy a home and ministry. If we are not on the same page, or if one rides roughshod over the other, it can be disastrous. Unresolved conflicts between parents and children can also derail us. When parents ignore their kids, it almost always comes back to haunt them. We've mentioned Eli and his troubles. David also provides an example of a family conflict that threw him off course. Think of his difficulties with Amnon, Tamar, and Absalom.

THE SPIRITUAL TEMPTATIONS OF OLD AGE

If these things are not enough to keep us from finishing well, consider some of the spiritual temptations that come our way as we enter the final quarter.

"What!" you say. "Do you mean we don't reach some stage as

a Christian where temptation stops and the spiritual battles are over?" I'm afraid not. At least, it hasn't yet happened at age 87! From what I read in my Bible, "no one is safe until they're home!"

One spiritual enemy of later old age is **fear and worry**. I've already talked a bit in chapter 3 about false worries, how I wake up in the night many times and find myself "building castles of worry." Questions trouble me: *How long will I live? How long can I provide? Did I do enough?* I become afraid. Then I catch myself, quote Scripture, and finally fall back to sleep. In the daytime, my number one worry-slayer habit is to read God's Word and then take it through the day with me (that's when I latch on to my SOS verses I told you about). I find that the fear of the Lord casts out and actually shrinks all my other lesser fears. Like the psalmist "I sought the Lord, and . . . he delivered me from all my fears" (Psalm 34:4).

In the end, a lot of what we worry about is a waste. I sometimes say to my children, "Most of the things you worry about never happen, and what does happen isn't as bad as you thought, and besides, no one is going to get out of this world alive anyway!" They laugh. But it's true!

Another spiritual enemy of old age is the **urge for security**. We keep thinking, *Am I secure enough?* Yes, we want to rightly meet our obligations. I want to provide for my wife and bless my family. But sometimes the "security thing" in us goes haywire. We crave security so much that we stop trusting in God, and we become less generous than we should. Worst of all, we forget the security that we have if we are in Christ.

Paul wrote to the Romans of God's deep love for us: "For I am convinced that neither death nor life, neither angels nor demons, neither the present nor the future, nor any powers, neither height nor depth, nor anything else in all creation, will be able to separate us from the love of God that is in Christ Jesus our Lord" (Romans 8:38–39).

One more enemy I am learning about is doubt. Now you might think that senior saints get beyond doubt. But we don't. It is so easy to forget God's goodness in the past—to forget everything in the past for that matter! It is easy to forget the promises of the gospel and to start trusting again in our own performance and ask, "Have I done enough?" It's easy to forget God's faithfulness over the years and fall into a kind of old-age depression and begin losing hope. Which is why, as I've said, we have to daily appropriate the gospel and recall that we are justified not by our works but by Christ's work, and that today we stand before God clothed in His righteousness.

All of these spiritual temptations and enemies can try to get us off track so that we do not finish well. So mark my word, if God gives you 80 years, you will still be fighting the good fight.

THE GOOD NEWS
ABOUT FINISHING WELL

But here is the good news. It is possible to follow Christ to the end of your life and finish well.

We've shared stories about some in our own day who have. There are also numerous examples in the Bible. My favorite is Paul. In Acts 20, Paul had his last meeting with the leaders of a church he planted in Ephesus. He loved these men. After reviewing his own ministry with them, he made a prediction. He said that the Holy Spirit had warned him that as soon as he gets to Jerusalem, prison and hardship await. Then he shared with them his aspiration and prayer. He said, "If only I may finish the race and complete the task the Lord Jesus has given me—the task of testifying to the gospel of God's grace" (Acts 20:24). So what happened?

Flash forward to the end of his life. We have his exact words in 2 Timothy. At this point he is most likely serving his second prison sentence in Rome. All that the Spirit warned of had come to pass. The journey hadn't been easy. But this is what he says: "I have fought the good fight, I have finished the race, I have kept the faith. Now there is in store for me the crown of righteousness, which the Lord, the righteous Judge, will award to me on that day—and not only to me, but also to all who have longed for his appearing" (2 Timothy 4:7–8).

Notice how he has finished. He will soon face his executioner. He sounds somewhat relieved that he has finally made it to the finish line, faith intact. He has finished well.

Did you catch the words "and not only to me"? This phrase signals that others, many others, will also get there and share in that same reward. This is good news!

HOW TO FINISH WELL

How then do we finish well? Much has been written about this topic in the past decade. We'd like to add a few of our own thoughts. So what does it take?

Let's start with grace. We finish well by the grace of God. That is also how we start the race. That is what keeps us in the race. And that is what takes us to the end. As John Newton put it in his famous hymn, "'Tis grace hath brought me safe thus far, and grace will lead me home."

When all is said and done, grace is the ultimate explanation for why any of us make it. We are kept by the grace of God. It is then very appropriate to pray, "Lord, give me the grace to finish well."

From this foundation, there is more to be said. We have observed six characteristics of those who finish well.

First, those who finish well have *a Christ-centered life.* They know they are saved by Him, and they never get over it. He is their life source. He is the center of their affections. As Graham Kendrick put it in a more recent hymn, they know "there is no greater joy" than knowing Him. Consequently, they focus more on loving Christ than avoiding sins. They know that a vibrant personal relationship with Jesus and a daily walk with Him are essential to everything. He is the spring from which comes all spiritual fruit. He is the vine; we draw our life from Him. When we plateau in our spiritual lives, we must come back to Him and seek renewal. Why? Because He is "the author and perfecter of our faith" (Hebrews 12:2).

Second, those who finish well have *a focused life.* They are focused first on Him, but second on the task that He has given to us. Call this the "focus factor!" They not only know the purpose of life (to know, love, serve, and glorify the Lord), but they also know the purpose of their lives. They have an accurate understanding of the gifts He has given them, the call He has given them, and often even the specific assignments He has for them.

They have a focused life and not a scattered life. Most people live scattered lives. They do not know the purpose of life, or the purpose for their lives. By contrast, those who finish well have a clarity of purpose and a constancy of purpose.

I (George) began to sense my own life purpose listening to different people preach at my church growing up. In the year 1941, there was a particular series of revival meetings. My wife and I went for forty-one nights straight, not missing an evening, listening to the preaching of evangelist George T. Stevens. It was there that we dedicated our lives to Christ to do whatever He wanted. I knew then that I was called to be an evangelist and Bible teacher. That is when I began preaching and drawing in public. I was a pretty good artist. A friend built me an easel. I would draw and then preach a Bible message. The local rescue missions in New York City and northern New Jersey would have me in—more for my drawing than for my preaching in those days. But I knew I was called to this ministry of evangelism and teaching. It was my life purpose. That has been my constant theme whether as an evangelist, pastor, or educator.

The phrase from Paul "this one thing I do" (Philippians 3:13 KJV) is very important in my life. It became my motto. Paul said, "this one thing I do," not "these fifty things I dabble in." That's because he had a focused life rather than a scattered one. It's a characteristic of those who finish well.

Third, those who end well have *disciplined lives.* That's the other side of being focused. To be focused, you have to eliminate the unnecessary.

To get this point across, the New Testament uses numerous athletic images. In 1 Corinthians 9, Paul pictures a runner. He said run in such a way that you may win. But then he added, "Every athlete exercises self-control in all things." Therefore he said, "I discipline my body and keep it under control, lest after preaching to others I myself should be disqualified" (vv. 25–27 ESV). The writer to the Hebrews said, "Since we are surrounded by such a great cloud of witnesses, let us throw off everything that hinders and the sin that so easily entangles, and let us run with perseverance the race marked out for us" (Hebrews 12:1). He too is talking about discipline.

A Christian who finishes well will practice spiritual disciplines. As Dallas Willard, Richard Foster, and others have enumerated, there will be the disciplines of abstinence such as fasting, silence, solitude, frugality, sacrifice, and chastity. But there will also be the disciplines of engagement such as prayer, fellowship, worship, study, service, confession, and submission.

These will help guard our inner lives. The disciplines will not become an end in themselves. For they are really disciplines in response to God's grace. Grace and discipline are spiritual friends, when kept in the right order. Spiritual disciplines become a means of grace that help us get to the finish line.

A fourth characteristic of those who finish well is that they have *a teachable spirit* through life. "Teachable" means that they maintain a humble posture and are open to receiving midcourse corrections. Those who finish well never stop doing this. They are lifelong learners. They learn from reading, from watching and listening to others, and from life itself. This keeps them from plateauing. Paul was like this. At the very end of his life, in the closing request of his last letter, he says to Timothy, "When you come . . . also bring my books" (2 Timothy 4:13 NLT). He was still learning and teachable, right to the very end. Amazing.

A fifth characteristic of those who finish well is that they have *a well-networked life.* We've written on this earlier, that you can't run this race alone. Success in the journey depends upon a network of key relationships. Those who finish well have had not just one but numerous mentors. There are people who pray for you. There is personal and group accountability. There is shepherding by pastors and encouragement by spiritual friends—co-travelers on the path to help you get there.

Sixth, along with all of these other traits, those who finish well have what I call *a lifelong perspective.* They try to take the long view of life—to look at things with the end in mind. This is not to say they didn't at times become disoriented or tempted to launch out on detours. All of us do that. But when tempted, certain life disciplines helped them stay on course.

John Stott told about how when he was appointed rector of All Souls at age 29, the urgent regularly crowded out the important. Events would often overtake him. Those of us who are in leadership know exactly what he's talking about. At one point, not far from a serious breakdown, he attended a pastors conference where one of the teachers said that every pastor should take a quiet day once a month to allow God to draw him up into His heart and mind—to look at his work from a divine perspective, focus on the important, and adjust his priorities accordingly.

This is exactly what Stott needed to be told. So he went through his diary and wrote the letter Q for quiet, one day a month. Someone got him a quiet room with meals so he could be alone. Only his secretary knew where he was. He would leave home early in the morning so he had ten to twelve hours in quiet.

Stott says he reserved for that day any matter that needed uninterrupted time. Yet he made sure there was time to pray and think about his own life and the life of the church. It was a season each month to seek God's mind and discern His priorities for the ministry. After beginning this discipline, Stott said, the burden of responsibility for the church was lifted from his shoulders. This monthly Q day became so valuable that eventually he had a Q day every week![1]

A Q day is only one way to regain this lifelong perspective. Others take minisabbaticals, or make sure there is some Sabbath rest built into their lives to listen to God. There are multiple ways to think about life with your end in view. The point is, do something to get this perspective. It will keep you from being sidetracked and give you an enlarged perspective.

Each of these characteristics play a part in helping us finish well—by God's grace, a Christ-centered life, a focused life, a disciplined life, a teachable life, a networked life, and a lifelong perspective. All play a part in our staying on track so we can finish our race. So that in the end we hear our master say, "Well done, good and faithful servant."

Do you long to hear those words?

A PRAYER TO FINISH WELL

Lord, strengthen me to finish well.

May I, as I draw closer to the end of my earthly life,
Be a man who loves Your Church more than I ever have,
A man who prays for Your Church and Your
    leaders in the church,
A man who shows his commitment to Your bride
    in all that I do.

Lord, strengthen me to finish well.

May I be a man of greater moral purity,
So indwelled in Your Word and in prayer,
That I am able to resist the temptations of
      the enemy,
That my life shines as an example for You to
      the watching world.

Lord, strengthen me to finish well.

May I be a man who loves my family more with
      each passing day,
A man more in love and dedicated to his wife,
A man who loves his adult children even more
      than I did when they were younger,
And a man who loves his grandchildren and
      generation to come.

Lord, strengthen me to finish well.

May I be a man who loves others more as I
      grow older,
A man who is less judgmental and more giving
      of grace,
A man who realizes that the plank in my own eye
      is large,
And that I should forgive even as You forgive me.

Lord, strengthen me to finish well.

May my life have greater joy with each day.
May I see the blessings of life and count them daily.
May I not grow older and more bitter,
But grow older rejoicing in You always.

Lord, strengthen me to finish well.

As the day draws closer when I meet You face to face,
May I be a man who was already drawing closer to You,
A man who eagerly anticipated that day,
And a man who left behind a legacy and not regrets.

Lord, strengthen me to finish well.

And then, and only then, can I say that my life was
     not lived in vain.[2]

By Thom Rainer, the president and CEO of LifeWay Christian Resources. He is
the author of twenty-one books, including *Simple Life*. Used with permission.

13

THE SOMBER SEASON

When Your Health Goes South

"EVEN THOUGH I WALK THROUGH
THE VALLEY OF THE SHADOW OF DEATH,
I WILL FEAR NO EVIL, FOR YOU ARE WITH ME."
—Psalm 23:4

FOR SOME REASON, both of us like movies where the hero goes out in flames. You know, like *Braveheart*, where William Wallace is fighting to the very end. Or *The Mission*, where the heroes go down holding the cross while being mowed down by gunfire. That's how we want to go.

But what if, at the end of our lives, we are called to walk through a different kind of valley of the shadow of death? What if we are led into a somber season where our health progressively falls apart and we never consciously make it to the runner's tape? How does that fit with finishing well?

AGING NOT SO GRACEFULLY

Recently a book came out called *Never Say Die: The Myth and Marketing of the New Old Age*, by Susan Jacoby. She writes about the myth of aging gracefully and describes the darker side of getting old. Yes, she says, we are living longer and staying healthier longer. But the time comes when that trajectory heads downward, not up. According to Jacoby, the general rule is that physical and financial hardships mount as people move beyond the relatively hardy 60s and 70s, now classified by sociologists as the "young old," and move into the harsher territory of the "old old" in the 80s and 90s. There is, she says, a fifty-fifty chance that anyone who survives to blow out 85 candles will endure years of significant mental or physical disability. The risk of Alzheimer's disease doubles every five years after age 65.

Jacoby writes, "I am about to present a portrait of advanced old age that some will find too pessimistic and negative."[1] She is out to puncture the balloon of the overly optimistic longevity movement. According to Jacoby, marketing has deceived the public by suggesting that the cures for our most serious diseases are imminent, including the cure for aging. She chides us, saying we have blind faith in medical solutions. Instead, we need to get over the fantasy that age can be defied and that we will soon discover the fountain of youth. The so-called age-defying products and services all come up short. Take enough supplements, apply enough wrinkle creams, have enough plastic surgeries and replacement parts, and, we are told, you can live well indefinitely. This, says Jacoby, is not how old age actually works.

We don't like to think about this. We always think we have a lot of time. Even at age 87, I (George) keep thinking that my decline is still way off.

But then comes that season when things break down. Complications mount. You have problems on top of problems. You have phlebitis plus hip problems. Or it's MS plus osteoporosis and bone fractures. Or you find out you have heart disease plus Parkinson's. Or it's not just prostate trouble but prostate trouble plus early onset Alzheimer's. There is a fall, followed by ministrokes.

Recently we heard about a motivational speaker who got dementia. So much for positive mental attitude. I also read about a faith-healing preacher with Alzheimer's. So much for "name it and claim it."

This is a season when dementia sometimes sets in and people's personalities appear to change. A godly mother starts to swear like a sailor! A dad becomes angry and mean. Adult children wonder, "What is happening to my parents?"

This is a season when PSA numbers go up, tumor markers rise, and biopsies, bone drips, and blood work come back with exactly the opposite news of what we long to hear.

What if we enter a time where troubles mount—pain increases, mobility decreases, and bowels don't function right? A season where there are too many doctor appointments, too many discouraging diagnoses, too many meds, and everything seems to be going in the wrong direction?

We've watched friends fight this stuff, but they don't seem to win. Then they get tired from all the treatments. Seasons like this can turn even the happiest disposition toward depression. Then what?

I (George) remember reading about one of my heroes, D. L. Moody. In the last years of his life, his difficulties multiplied. He was considerably overweight and couldn't get the pounds off. His one-year-old grandson, his namesake, died in 1898. Nine months later his granddaughter Irene, whom he also adored, passed away. Along with this deep grief, he wasn't feeling well in late 1899.

Friends observed that the great preacher had added some thirty pounds to his already ample frame. His complications of being overweight put great pressure on his heart. While preaching at a series of meetings in Kansas City, for the first time he had to call it quits. He preached his last sermon on November 16 and quickly returned home to Northfield, Massachusetts, by train. Most people believe he was dying from congestive heart failure. By December 22, he was gone.

That was 1899. Over one hundred years later, because of the wonders of modern medicine, we are living longer—but we are also dying longer. In the United States during the twentieth century, we have seen the major causes of death change. In the first half of the century, the challenge was quick-killing infectious disease or heart attacks and stroke. But as the century wore on, death rates from heart attack dropped dramatically.

Now it is more common for death to advance more slowly. Chronic illnesses mean that dying often takes longer. Physicians speak of "gradual dying." The leading causes of death progress more slowly. According to a Rand Health white paper, most elderly Americans are diagnosed with a disease three years before dying.[2] Thirty-five percent of the elderly will die in nursing homes. Dying like this is not in anyone's plans, yet it happens more often than we realize.[3]

A NAME FOR THIS SEASON?

So what do we call this unexpected season? Is this "the winter of discontent"? Is it the final hardship before release?

Is it the age of extreme feebleness, as Charles Wesley wrote?

The great hymn writer, who died of old age in 1788, penned these words near the end of his life:

> In age and feebleness extreme, who shall a sinful
>   worm redeem?
> Jesus, my only hope thou art, strength of my
>   failing flesh and heart;
> Oh, could I catch a smile from thee, and drop
>   into eternity![4]

One hears in his words exasperation—although a hopeful exasperation!

Do we refer to this season as "sad and sinking times"? This is a phrase used by English Puritan preacher Jeremiah Burroughs to describe the hardships of his own day in his classic book *The Rare Jewel of Christian Contentment.* He used this arresting phrase to refer to all those conditions, personal and societal, that are prone to discourage the Christian and leave us discontent.

We will refer to this period of life as "the somber season"— a season at the end of life over which we have little control. It is a season of letting go, a winter of dependence and decline—a time of easy discouragement. How long will it last? It's hard to know. For some it is months, for others a year or two, for still others it may last a decade or more.

When John Bunyan wrote the Christian classic *Pilgrim's Progress*, people generally died young. Life expectancy was about 35! For the most part, death approached quickly. Bunyan's main characters do not get hit with a terminal disease and go into a slow, steady decline in health.

One wonders what Christian's or Christiana's journeys would look like if he wrote his classic in 2012.

A PLAN FOR THIS SEASON

In describing this unexpected season, we're not claiming to know exactly why this happens (aside from the normal biblical explanations) or why it happens to some people and not others. Nor do we know what it is like to go through it, apart from watching loved ones and friends who have traveled down this harder path. But we have given some thought to what it takes to get through a season like this. It takes at least three mental and spiritual attitudes. And that is what we turn to for the rest of this chapter.

Humility and Courage

First, it takes humility and courage. This season is not for the faint of heart. It can be medicated, but it can't be stopped. How will you respond?

I have friend who is a hospice worker. She tells me that people seem to approach this taxing season with one of two attitudes. Some approach it with an open hand and are willing to let go. Others approach it with a shaking fist. They are full of rage or bitterness.

Some time ago, I (Don) was with an elderly relative. When I would ask him how he was doing, he would usually complain and moan. There was always deep cynicism in his words. One time he looked at me and said, "It is hell to be 93." But for him, it was "hell" to be 90, 91, and 92. He was cynical about everything.

By contrast, many of us will never forget former president Ronald Reagan in his postpresidential years (1989–2004). Reagan was not only the oldest elected president (at age 69), but he was also one of the oldest living ex-presidents (at age 93).

In August 1994, when he was 83, he was diagnosed with Alzheimer's disease. Rather than deny it or hide it, he went public and informed the nation in a letter what was happening to him. He wrote:

> I have recently been told that I am one of the millions of Americans who will be afflicted with Alzheimer's Disease . . . At the moment I feel just fine. I intend to live the remainder of the years God gives me on this earth doing the things I have always done . . . I now begin the journey that will lead me into the sunset of my life. I know that for America there will always be a bright dawn ahead. Thank you, my friends. May God always bless you.[5]

His action and words not only showed humility (here was one who had been the most powerful man in the world now willing to let go), but it also showed enormous courage. His attitude encouraged many others to face their own difficult seasons with this incurable neurological disorder.

Even if you are not some dignitary, the somber season will humble you. It is filled with the indignities of failing health. There is a stripping away. You've not only let go of many of the things of your life, but now you are letting go of your health—your body as you knew it. You!

On top of this there is often obscurity. If you live that long, many of your loved ones will already be gone. Few will miss you in a nursing home.

But for some people, this stripping away is not the whole story. They know that our life story and our journey involve two aspects: descent and ascent. We are in Christ who goes before us. Our journey finds its meaning and significance in His. That's why for some people, in the stripping of the somber season, hope burns more brightly—if they are spiritually prepared for what is to come.

Unfortunately, not all are prepared. Some have only a theology of descent. For them, decline and descent capture the whole story. Others have only a theology of ascent. They have the resurrection in view but have forgotten the way of the cross.

Yet in Christ, both are essential parts of the story. Jesus' journey involved two aspects: descent and ascent, subtraction and addition. In fact, all history is moving along this pattern, including our history!

In Philippians 2, we have a clear picture of this. Verses 5–11 speak of Christ's own humiliation and exaltation. As the One who is God, He humbles Himself to become a servant, but then humbles Himself and becomes "obedient to death" (v. 8). He knows the path that has been marked out for Him. But this is not the whole story. God then "exalted him to the highest place" (v. 9). Do you see both aspects? The passage is prefaced by verse 5, which says, "Your attitude should be the same as that of Christ Jesus." But then it is followed by the words, "Do everything without complaining or arguing, so that you may become blameless and pure, children of God without fault in a crooked and depraved generation, in which you shine like stars in the universe as you hold out the word of life" (vv. 14–16).

As Christ and His Word shape us, that changes our attitudes so we can face the future with humility and courage.

Planning and Care

A second mind-set that can help us prepare for the somber season is one of planning and care. We see so many families approach this season of life without this. In fact, we see too many families who don't seem to care at all.

You heard about the woman from Brooklyn who turned 80? On her big birthday she decided to prepare her last will and testament. So she went to her pastor to make two final requests. First, she insisted on cremation.

"What's your second request?" the pastor asked.

"I want my ashes scattered over Bloomingdale's."

The pastor said, "But why Bloomingdale's?"

The woman replied, "Then I'll be sure that my daughters will visit me twice a week!"

We laugh, but it's no laughing matter. Many parents are left to enter this season on their own. We saw a recent news story where in Oakland, California, a 62-year-old man who could neither walk nor talk was found abandoned on a flight from El Paso, Texas. A note was pinned to his clothing, saying that he needed medical attention.[6]

Whatever happened to "Honor your father and mother"? God instructs us to care for our parents and even attaches promises of longevity to those who heed His command. "Honor your father and your mother," the commandment says, "so that you may live long in the land the Lord your God is giving you" (Exodus 20:12).

What do we mean by approaching this season with the mind-set of planning and care? It means we will plan for the end of life by initiating conversations that address end-of-life issues. With sensitivity but definiteness, we will bring up the uncomfortable topics long before we need to act on them. But be warned, these will be some of the hardest conversations you will ever have. Yet having them is an act of care itself, and thinking them through is a part of finishing well!

We have already talked in a previous chapter about funerals. Here are some other questions you will want to talk about as a family. We encourage you to get input from your doctor, your family, and your pastor.

- Do you have a will?
- How do you want your assets to be disbursed?
- Are there life insurance policies?
- How and where do you want to live when independence is no longer possible?
- If you lose your independence, what are your financial and family resources to support an assisted-living arrangement?
- What are your end-of-life care wishes?
- Are there living wills or advanced directives?
- What do you want your last days to look like? Do you want to die in a hospital or at home in a comfortable and familiar place?
- What medical directives do you want in place for your last days?
- What principles do you want to guide the people who are caring for you?

With this information in hand, it is good if wise family members can put together a family care plan. Family members will have to ask themselves: How can we prolong our parents' independence? And when our parents lose their independence, then what? What are the resources available from all sources, and what are our options?

Once a family care plan is agreed upon, the actual "caring through presence" takes place. You just need to be there or have someone who cares be there. They need to be checked up on, called, and included in events as much as possible. They will need to be helped in the things they can no longer do for themselves—in cooking, cleaning, taking care of personal hygiene, even using the bathroom. This is what it means to love a dying parent or friend.

This all might sound earthy and hard, and it is. Nevertheless, behind it all is a biblical mandate of care for families reflected not only in God's Ten Commandments but also in passages like 1 Timothy 5:8, where Paul says, "If anyone does not provide for his relatives, and especially for members of his household, he has denied the faith and is worse than an unbeliever" (ESV). Strong words, but relevant to our circumstances.

Waiting and Trust

Getting through this season will take humility and courage. It will take planning and care. Let's mention one final mind-set that can help us prepare for the somber season. Getting through will require waiting and trust.

How long must we wait? We can't say. We have a dear friend who had an incapacitating stroke in his 60s, and now in his 80s he is still waiting, still trusting that God will care for him and meet him on the other side.

Some months before John Stott died, a friend was telling me about a final visit with him. By this time Dr. Stott had given up international travel. He had already preached his last sermon. He had written his last book. His health was progressively failing. He was clearly in the somber season. He used a walker. His sight was going. Ministrokes had destroyed his ability to do things.

He kept meeting with people and even took some calls, advising the Lausanne Committee and the Langham Partnership. But even that was winding down. His mind was still very active, but he was not able to lift his head and was slumped over, having a hard time holding himself up. Can you imagine a person of such influence being reduced to that—imprisoned by his own body? Yet in this visit, the man reported, Dr. Stott said, "Read 2 Corinthians 4 and 5 to me!" So the friend read these words:

Therefore we do not lose heart. Though outwardly we are wasting away, yet inwardly we are being renewed day by day. For our light and momentary troubles are achieving for us an eternal glory that far outweighs them all. So we fix our eyes not on what is seen, but on what is unseen. For what is seen is temporary, but what is unseen is eternal.

Now we know that if the earthly tent we live in is destroyed, we have a building from God, an eternal house in heaven, not built by human hands. Meanwhile we groan, longing to be clothed with our heavenly dwelling, because when we are clothed, we will not be found naked. For while we are in this tent, we groan and are burdened, because we do not wish to be unclothed but to be clothed with our heavenly dwelling, so that what is mortal may be swallowed up by life. Now it is God who has made us for this very purpose and has given us the Spirit as a deposit, guaranteeing what is to come.

Therefore we are always confident and know that as long as we are at home in the body we are away from the Lord. We live by faith, not by sight. We are confident, I say, and would prefer to be away from the body and at home with the Lord. (2 Corinthians 4:16–5:8)

As the passage was read, Dr. Stott was clearly following along. It was a passage he knew well, and now it was filled with precious hope. He was clearly revealing a mind-set of waiting and trust. Because he knew that the somber season would soon pass, and there would be glory . . . on the other side.

14

DYING WELL AND THE BLESSING OF A GOOD DEATH

"PREPARE ME FOR DEATH, THAT I MAY NOT DIE AFTER
LONG AFFLICTION OR SUDDENLY, BUT AFTER SHORT
ILLNESS, WITH NO CONFUSION OR DISORDER,
AND A QUIET DISCHARGE IN PEACE,
WITH ADIEU TO BRETHREN."[1]
—*A PURITAN PRAYER*

THE PHRASES "dying well" and "good death" sound outlandish in our culture, for all sorts of reasons. The phrases come across as oxymoronic. Dying well? Good death? How so? For those who believe this life is all there is, they wonder—how can death be good if it involves the cessation of all that we know? Even Christians who hear the phrases often reject them because they are quite sure that death is always an enemy. So, dying well? Good death? No, they say. It is not possible.

Earlier generations of Christians beg to differ. For some in the early church, dying well meant imitating Christ and following in the likeness of His death. So they aspired to martyrdom. Not the kind with explosives attached to their belts. Rather, they aspired to be a faithful Christian witness, no matter what the cost. If that meant death, so be it. That was the way to die well. After all, did not Jesus say, "The man who loves his life will lose it, while the man who hates his life in this world will keep it for eternal life" (John 12:25). Early church leader Clement of Alexandria wrote, "The church is full of those persons—chaste women as well as men—who all of their life have contemplated the death that rouses up to Christ." Such martyrs, he believed, rejoice in heaven because they have perfected their testimony in the confession of the Savior.[2]

In the Middle Ages, many European Christians hoped for a good death too. As they were threatened by disease, famine, and the constant presence of war, death was a brutal part of most people's everyday life. There was no Social Security, no life insurance. For them, a good death was one where they slowly but consciously departed this world with a priest administering last rites. Sudden death, on the other hand, was a bad death. It was greatly feared because there was no way to prepare for it and confess remaining sins. A lack of preparation would lengthen their time in purgatory. So they thought.

Christians of the Reformation era, and Puritans after them, talked frequently about dying well. They experienced much persecution, losing many creature comforts because of their faith. They thought a lot about the transitory nature of this life. This life, many of them believed, is a preparation for the next life. Calvin said it is nothing but a lobby or a front entrance, a vestibule, for the next life.[3] The Puritan vision of dying well was to die consciously and alert. They would listen to and often record their loved ones' words as they moved toward heaven. They prayed, not for a "long affliction" or a "sudden death" but rather for a fully alert death surrounded by close friends.

They are like Mr. Standfast in Bunyan's *Pilgrim's Progress*, as he went down into the river of death. When he was about halfway in, Bunyan says, he stood for a while and talked with his companions who were with him.[4]

In our day, many Christians view a good death as one where you can be productive for Christ to the very end. Perhaps no other person embodied this more than Bill Bright, who died in 2003.

Bright was the visionary, entrepreneurial leader of Campus Crusade for Christ (now Cru). In his journey from Oklahoma to California to Florida, he left the business world to obey the Great Commission. He and his amazing wife, Vonette, raised up an army of personal evangelists, challenging them to be willing to go anywhere, do anything, and say anything for the cause of Christ. In the process, Bright grew what has been called "the world's largest Christian ministry." Both of us knew Bill Bright and had him visit our churches.

The final stage of Bright's pilgrimage was not easy. He was diagnosed with pulmonary fibrosis, a dreadful disease in which lungs eventually lose their elasticity. Death comes by slow suffocation. Nevertheless, he maintained a buoyant spirit. As he battled the disease, he continued to work. He told Chuck Colson that the last two years of his life had been the most productive in his ministry, where he was able to write more, direct more projects, and launch more initiatives than ever before. Colson recalls, "He kept praising God even as he was gasping for the breath" to describe his final efforts in this world. He wanted to go the distance and keep serving Christ to the very end.[5]

In some ways, Bright was like John Wesley. When Wesley was asked by a friend, "Suppose you knew that you were to die by midnight tomorrow, John. How would you spend your time until then?"

Wesley replied, "I would spend it exactly as I expect to spend it now. I would preach tonight in Gloucester. I would get up early tomorrow and proceed to Tewkesbury, where I would preach in the afternoon. Then I would go to the Martins' house in the evening, since they are expecting me. I would talk with Mr. Martin and pray with the family. Upon retiring to my room at ten o'clock, I would put myself in the Father's care, go to sleep, and wake up in glory."[6]

For Christians, dying well means more than death without pain or suffering. It certainly means a whole lot more than those who use the phrase "good death" to refer to assisted suicide! Christians believe one can only die well because of the resurrection of Jesus Christ. Good death is only possible through Christ, who has defeated death. In Christ, death's sting has been removed.

HOW SHOULD CHRISTIANS VIEW DEATH: AS AN ENEMY OR A FRIEND?

So how should Christians look at death? Let's think about this for a moment.

First of all, we should think of death as an enemy. According to the Genesis account, death does not appear to be part of God's original good creation. When He made us, we were created to live. So there is something about death that is not natural and very wrong. When it comes, death arrives as a disruptive intruder. It brings great anxiety and fear. The fear of death in Scripture is viewed as a kind of terror or slavery that holds sway over people (Hebrews 2:15).

Death brings destruction. As pastors who have watched

disease eat away the very flesh of people we love, we can say with conviction that we hate death. We have experienced its harsh reality many times. We have felt the pain of separation that it brings and have been touched by the complexities of grief. It is our enemy. In 1 Corinthians 15:25–26, death is described as "the last enemy to be destroyed" when Christ puts all His enemies under His feet.

The harsh reality of death came among us, according to Scripture, because of Adam and Eve's sinful disobedience. It is a sign of God's wrath toward sinners. Death separates, and this separation is a part of our curse. Spiritual death separates us from God. Physical death separates body and soul. Death separates us from loved ones. Its power breaks apart all kinds of things. Though it is a defeated enemy for us, it is still an enemy that we rightly try to hold at bay in the normal course of life.

But that is not all Scripture says about death! Biblically, death has another role. By God's grace, death is more than an enemy. It is also a strange mercy. It was that way in the beginning. Death came that we might not live forever in our sin (Genesis 3:22).

Death is also a calling—a sacred calling, if you will. According to Ecclesiastes 3:1–3, "There is a time for everything, and a season for every activity under heaven." This includes both "a time to be born and a time to die." This passage suggests a divinely ordained time—that our times really are in His hands (Psalm 31:15). Hebrews 9:27 echoes this in telling us that it is "appointed" or "destined" for men to die. Some say God has nothing to do with death. But they forget that Christ holds the keys of death (Revelation 1:17–18) and that the God who has numbered our days is sovereign over death.

Death is also a blessing or "friend" in the sense that in Christ, it becomes the gateway into His eternal presence. Charles Spurgeon called it "the gate of life," a waiting room where we robe ourselves for immortality.[7] We leave this life of sin and enter into the presence of Christ. In that sense, it "is gain" because we are with the Lord, which, as Paul says, is better by far (2 Corinthians 5:6; Philippians 1:20–23).

Because of this blessing, Christians through the ages have referred to death in what might seem like strange language, unless it is seen through Christ's resurrection. Believers have referred to death as ultimate healing. When we die in Christ, health is not something we die out of but something that we die into! Healing comes after death. Death brings us there.

Christians have also referred to their death as a kind of birthday. They compare the labor of dying to that of birth. There is a miracle in a good death just as there is a miracle in a good birth. Medieval writers such as John Donne and even the great reformer Martin Luther wrote about this. In Luther's "A Sermon on Preparing to Die," he said, "Just as an infant is born with peril and pain from the small abode of its mother's womb into this immense heaven and earth . . . so man departs this life through the narrow gate of death . . . Therefore the death of the dear saints is called a new birth, and their feast day is known in Latin as *natale*, that is the day of their birth!"[8]

Medieval writers celebrated the anniversary of a martyr's death for Christ. It was known as their birth day—a birth into everlasting life. Some spoke of our three birthdays—when we are born, when we are born again, and when we are born into eternal life!

In our family, there has been a long emphasis on the second coming of the Lord. We have been second-coming Christians, longing for the blessed hope of Christ's return. We believe in watching and praying and waiting for it. Yet as we continue to wait, so far, He has not returned. That will happen! But to this point in church history, the way He returns for us is at our death.

You could say there are two ways that He will come again. "He will come again in glory to judge the quick and the dead" as the Apostles' Creed says. And we would like to live until He does.

But if He doesn't come for us corporately in our lifetime, He will come for us individually, just as He did for Stephen in Acts 7:59 when, as they were stoning him, he cried out, "Lord Jesus, receive my spirit."

So which is it? What is death's true face? Is death an enemy or a friend? Is it a curse or a blessing? The paradox of death is that for the believer it has two faces. While it remains our enemy, by grace through faith, the curse becomes a blessing through Christ. So then, for the believer there is such a thing as a good death. It is possible to die well.

THE ART OF DYING

Now the question remains: How does one die well? Through this book we have talked about various ways to finish well. We've mentioned things such as thinking of life as a long-distance journey, applying the gospel all the way through, and loving the people around us.

In the rest of this chapter, we'd like to complete the picture. There are still a few more things that need to be said. Let's try to summarize it in five statements.

1. People who die well are preoccupied with the desire to live well.

The real secret of a good death is a good life! People who die well keep going as long as they can, thankful for each day but with a resolve to make every one count. They persevere in faith. They are aware of death but not consumed by it. They are awake to the Lord, and to the people around them, and they seek to be a channel of His blessing. Whether by martyrdom or normal service, they are focused on serving Christ to the end of their days, being a faithful witness and a faithful presence for Him. So many of the heroes of faith we have described in this book, the pacesetters, have modeled this kind of life. That's why we believe that the real secret of dying well is found in looking at each day as a gift from God—and resolving to live it to the fullest for His glory.

2. People who die well think about their death long before it happens.

Instead of living in constant denial of death, they repeatedly take it into consideration.

These days, so many people go to great lengths to evade death. The dying are removed from our homes. We do not hear their cries because they cry in some hospital room far away.

In previous generations people had constant reminders of death. Paintings would commonly have a skull or bones in them to remind the viewer that soon they too would die. These reminders were referred to as *memento mori*, a Latin phrase meaning, "Remember that you must die." They served as telling reminders of our mortality and the judgment soon to come.

The great American theologian and pastor Jonathan Edwards

at age 19 famously resolved to think much, on all occasions, of his own dying.[9] Why? So that he might live his life in light of that day. He knew that only by facing the reality of his coming death would he become fully alive.

The time to contemplate death is not when you face your last hour but long before that, so you are ready.

3. People who die well know where they are going when they die. They have a growing assurance of their salvation.

They know the truth of verses such as John 3:16: "For God so loved the world that he gave his one and only Son, that whoever believes in him shall not perish but have eternal life." They have confessed their sins and repented of them before a holy but loving God. They have put their faith in Christ and His righteousness. They rely on the work of His atoning death for the forgiveness of their sins. They believe in the resurrection of Jesus and in His power to raise us up to new life. They know the truth of John 1:12, that "to all who received him, to those who believed in his name, he gave the right to become children of God."

They begin to bear fruit, and as they do, they have the confirming witness of the Spirit. But they also understand this—that we can know that we have peace with God. That, as 1 John 5:12–13 says, "He who has the Son has life; he who does not have the Son of God does not have life." But these things were written in the Bible "so that you may know that you have eternal life."

People who die well know where they are going when death comes. They have such a firm relationship with the Lord that, despite the hardships of dying, they persevere to the end and die in hope.

Occasionally my dad would go around the table at dinnertime and ask each of the children if we knew where we were going when we died. He wanted us to be sure and to put our faith in Christ.

4. People who die well seek guidance about when to cease striving for a cure and when to confidently embrace death as God's calling.

They talk with family, with doctors and spiritual caregivers about what is the right next step in their treatment. But most of all they seek the guidance of the Good Shepherd who leads us, even through the valley of the shadow of death.

End-of-life issues can be complex due to the amazing advances in medical technology. Our physical life can be extended by all kinds of artificial and extraordinary means.

Neither one of us is qualified to advise on such medical issues. For a physician's point of view of these things, we recommend a book like *Finishing Well to the Glory of God: Strategies from a Christian Physician,* by John Dunlop, MD.

But as pastors, we have observed many people with serious illness. We know that doctors can err on the side of overtreatment, sometimes for liability reasons. There are appropriate life-sustaining treatments. But there are also times when such measures go beyond faith or reason. We've seen too many congregants, after conventional measures have failed, placed on experimental treatments and drugs with little chance of success. In the end, these individuals were robbed of time to prepare to die.

Sometimes in our unwillingness to let go, we encourage doctors to do "everything possible"—and that is exactly what they will do.

People who die well ask appropriate questions. Can health be restored? Is a cure really possible? What is the natural course this sickness will take—with and without treatment?

How risky are the treatments? What is the record of success? Are there complications? How hard are these treatments on the body? Will they obliterate any quality of life at the end? Are we placing our hope in medical technology or God and His ultimate healing? Should we hang on, or is God calling us home?

These are not easy questions, but they are necessary questions. People who die well know when to stop striving for a cure and when to confidently embrace death as God's calling—as a gateway to what He has next for them. Once we know this time has come, it is wise to focus on comfort, our loved ones, and our Savior into whose arms we must soon fall. Like Christians of old, many people still covet a final respite at the end of life, to have time to die and prepare for the next step of the journey.

When the great British preacher and former physician D. Martyn Lloyd-Jones was at the end of his life, he was being kept alive by medical technology. He is reported to have said to his doctors, "You are keeping me from the glory!"[10]

5. Finally, people who die well are surrounded by friends who remind them of their hope in Christ.

They do not die alone. When facing death's power, they find support in the fellowship and faith of the church. It has been said that the experience of dying, while intensely personal, can't be faced privately without our being crushed. For this reason it is good to be surrounded by loved ones. Hospice workers testify that one of the most important factors that makes for a good death is the enriching presence of loved ones with the patient. The ministry of a quiet presence goes a long way. We must not abandon someone and let them die alone.

When John Stott died, he was surrounded by friends and music from Handel's *Messiah*, with the words of "I Know My Redeemer Liveth" in his ears. We have stood around many a deathbed, singing psalms, hymns, or spiritual songs of hope. Though the person dying did not always appear to be conscious, they are often spiritually awake.

One time, I (Don) remember singing a hymn around the deathbed of a dear saint. We were told he had slipped into a coma. We read Scripture, sang, and prayed. When we finished singing, we put a hymnbook down on the table next to the bed and were ready to walk out. At which point, and to our shock, the supposedly unconscious man with eyes apparently closed, grabbed the hymnal and lifted it up as a signal for us to keep singing!

People crossing the river of death need to be assured of the love of friends and the hope of the gospel. They need to know that death will not have the last word, and that, in the words of the old French hymn, "It is not death to die."

> It is not death to die,
> To leave this weary road,
> And midst the brotherhood on high
> To be at home with God.
>
> It is not death to close
> The eye long dimmed by tears,
> And wake, in glorious repose,
> To spend eternal years.

It is not death to bear
The wrench that sets us free
From dungeon chain, to breathe the air
Of boundless liberty.

It is not death to fling
Aside this sinful dust
And rise, on strong exulting wing
To live among the just.

Jesus, Thou Prince of Life,
Thy chosen cannot die:
Like Thee, they conquer in the strife
To reign with Thee on high.

It is not death to die
To leave this weary road
And join the saints who dwell on high
Who've found their home with God.

It is not death to close
The eyes long dimmed by tears
And wake in joy before Your throne
Delivered from our fears.

O Jesus, conquering the grave
Your precious blood has power to save
Those who trust in You

Will in Your mercy find
That it is not death to die.

It is not death to fling
Aside this earthly dust
And rise with strong and noble wing
To live among the just.

It is not death to hear
The key unlock the door
That sets us free from mortal years
To praise You evermore.[11]

15

IN CHRIST THE BEST IS YET TO BE

Eternal Joys and Lasting Pleasures

"WHEN JOHN OWEN, THE GREAT PURITAN THEOLO-
GIAN AND CHURCH LEADER, LAY ON HIS DEATHBED,
HIS SECRETARY WROTE IN HIS NAME TO A FRIEND,
'I AM STILL IN THE LAND OF THE LIVING.' 'STOP,'
SAID OWEN. 'CHANGE THAT AND SAY, "I AM YET
IN THE LAND OF THE DYING, BUT I HOPE SOON
TO BE IN THE LAND OF THE LIVING." ' "[1]
—*PULPIT DIGEST*

SO WHAT IS THE END of the journey for the Christian?
After we go through death, what do we come to on the other side?
And what do we mean by this word "heaven"?

John Bunyan's monumental classic, *Pilgrim's Progress*, consists
of many journeys, not just one.

There is Christian's journey, but then in part 2, there is his
wife, Christiana's, journey. There are others who are pilgrims
as well. The main characters all come to the end of their earthly
journey and approach the Celestial City. But before they get
there, they must cross the dark river of death. Each person's

crossing is somewhat different. Here is a snippet from part 2, describing Mr. Standfast's venture to the other side.

When Mr. Standfast had thus set things in order, and the time being come for him to haste him away, he also went down to the river. Now there was a great calm at that time in the river; wherefore Mr. Stand-fast, when he was about half-way in, stood a while and talked to his companions that had waited upon him thither; and he said,

This river has been a terror to many; yea, the thoughts of it also have often frightened me.

But now, methinks, I stand easy, my foot is fixed upon that upon which the feet of the priests that bare the ark of the covenant stood, while Israel went over this Jordan (Josh. 3:17). The waters, indeed, are to the palate bitter, and to the stomach cold; yet the thoughts of what I am going to, and of the conduct that waits for me on the other side, doth lie as a glowing coal at my heart.

I see myself now at the end of my journey, my toilsome days are ended. I am going now to see that Head that was crowned with thorns, and that Face that was spit upon for me.

I have formerly lived by hearsay and faith; but now I go where I shall live by sight, and shall be with Him in whose company I delight myself.

I have loved to hear my Lord spoken of; and wherever I have seen the print of His shoe in the earth, there I have coveted to set my foot too. . . .

Now, while he was thus in discourse, his countenance changed, his strong man bowed under him; and after he had said, Take me, for I come unto Thee, he ceased to be seen of them. But glorious it was to see how the open region was filled with horses and chariots, with trumpeters and pipers, with singers and players on stringed instruments, to welcome the Pilgrims as they went up, and followed one another in at the beautiful gate of the city.[2]

Bunyan's book is only an allegory. It was written long ago, in the 1600s, so the language may be a bit challenging. And the picture it-self is different from the one that we might be used to. There is no rapture mentioned. There is no intermediate state. There's no mil-lennium. His principle concern is what comes at the very end. And that is our concern in this chapter as well. What is this heaven at the end of our journey—the Christian's journey?

WHAT IS HEAVEN?

Some say heaven is a hoax. The famous scientist Stephen Hawking claims that heaven "is a fairy story for people afraid of the dark."[3]

Others picture heaven like Maria Shriver did in her children's book *What's Heaven?* The book is described as a treasure book for people of all faiths. According to Shriver, when you die, you leave earth and go to heaven, which is a beautiful place where you can sit on soft clouds and talk.[4]

Still others will take one dominant biblical image of heaven and focus exclusively on heaven being a place of splendorous beauty, or a mansion with many rooms, or a promised land where we are finally free, or a place of eternal rest, or a reunion of the redeemed, or a place of ongoing growth and service.

What exactly does the word "heaven" mean?

First of all, when Scripture speaks about heaven, it sometimes is referring to the physical heavens we see every day. In Genesis 1:1 it refers to the entire cosmos: "In the beginning God created the heavens and the earth." But then it also refers to the expanse that He called "sky" (Genesis 1:8). This is where birds fly and clouds float. It is also where He placed the stars. These are all unworthy of our worship, because God made them. But God Himself is so great that the heavens cannot contain Him (1 Kings 8:27).

At other times when the Bible speaks of heaven, it refers to God Himself. One thinks of the parable of the lost son, when the wayward son comes to his senses and says to his father, "I have sinned against heaven and against you" (Luke 15:21). "Heaven" here refers to God. We find the same thing in the Gospels when Matthew uses the phrase "kingdom of heaven" while Mark and John use the phrase "kingdom of God." Matthew is writing for a Jewish audience. It was their practice to avoid using God's name because it was so holy. So "heaven" stands for "God."

Another use of the term "heaven" in the Bible refers to a real spiritual place or dimension.

It is the place where God dwells—where He is enthroned (Exodus 24:9–11; Isaiah 66:1; Matthew 6:9). God is the God of heaven (Jonah 1:9). He is not alone there, because the hosts of heaven worship Him (Nehemiah 9:6). Heaven is where Jesus came from (John 3:13; 6:33 ff.), and where after His resurrection He would return (Acts 1:11). Christ is now in heaven. He has promised to return from heaven to earth.

The blessed reside in heaven. It is, as Calvin said, "our father land." Compared to that, he said, "what else is this world but a grave" because we live in the land of the dying.[5] C. S. Lewis's writings often picture heaven as our true home as well; it is the land we have been searching for our whole lives. Meanwhile we live in the shadowlands.

This spiritual place called heaven is sometimes identified as the location of "the intermediate state." That is, the time in between—where the righteous go after their death and before the resurrection of their bodies.

At death there is a separation. Because of sin, the soul is violently torn from the body. Our bodies are laid in the ground and return to dust (Genesis 3:19). They are resting and await resurrection day.

Where do the souls of the righteous go? They immediately go to be with the Lord. On the cross, Jesus said to one of the thieves crucified with Him, "Today you will be with me in paradise" (Luke 23:43). He would go to heaven that very day.

While Paul was looking forward to resurrection day, he knew that "as long as we are at home in the body we are away from the Lord" (2 Corinthians 5:6). Then he added, "We are confident, I say, and would prefer to be away from the body and at home with the Lord" (v. 8). In saying this, he was not renouncing the body. The text makes that very plain. He was just longing to be with Christ. He says the same thing in his letter to the Philippians: "For to me, to live is Christ and to die is gain" (1:21). Living meant more fruitful labor for Paul. But dying meant departing and being with Christ, which, he says, is far better.

That reminds us of a comment D. L. Moody made near the end of his life, on that last preaching campaign in Kansas City. He said,

"Some day you will read in the papers that D. L. Moody of East Northfield is dead. Don't believe a word of it! At that moment I shall be more alive than I am now!"[6]

For the believer in Christ, death is a departure from the body—not into nothingness but into the presence of the Lord. It is a time when our souls retain their natural faculties in a conscious existence—hearing, speaking, thinking. They join with "thousands upon thousands" of angels in joyful assembly, and with "the spirits of righteous men made perfect" in the heavenly Jerusalem worshiping their Lord (Hebrews 12:22–23).

John also wrote of this in Revelation 6:9. When the Lamb of God opens the fifth seal, John sees under the altar "the souls of those who had been slain because of the word of God and the testimony they had maintained." They are conscious and speaking to the Sovereign Lord, longing for the day of final justice.

Again, this is a real picture of heaven now. But it is not the final heaven. It is an intermediate state where the spirits of those who are saved go.

But this is not the only place where spirits go at death. The souls of the defiant are cast into Hades and there await both the resurrection of the body and the final judgment (Luke 16:23 ff.; Acts 1:25). Like eternal hell, this Hades is a real place, only it involves separation from God and others, deep regret, and exposure to the wrath of God. It too is a place of punishment. But it is not technically hell. Because Revelation 20:14 says that death and Hades, in the end, will be thrown into the lake of fire, and this is the second death.

The point is, there is a vast difference between the future of the righteous and the wicked. There is no question more important than where we will spend eternity. Jesus came to save so that people would not perish but have everlasting life (John 3:16).

Make no mistake, as unpopular a subject as it is, hell cannot be wished away. If there is a heaven, then there is a place that is not heaven. In the Bible, the heights of paradise are contrasted by the depths of the abyss, just as the greatness of salvation is contrasted by the awfulness of being unrescued.

The reason Christians have believed in hell as much as we believe in heaven is primarily because Jesus did. In His preaching He consistently and repeatedly uses the most graphic images to warn people about hell's awful reality (Matthew 8:11–12; 13:41–42; Mark 9:42–48; Luke 16:22–24).

The reason Christians believe in hell is not because we are vindictive but because God is just and holy—as well as loving. His love does not swallow up His justice and righteousness. Or as Paul put it, the kindness of God does not negate the severity of God (Romans 11:22). We are to leave room in our theology for God's wrath as well as His love, because it is the Lord who says, "It is mine to avenge; I will repay" (Romans 12:19).

Images of hell in Scripture are terrifying and are meant to shock us. The reality of separation from God's goodness and presence is pictured by darkness and banishment. The ruin and loss experienced in hell are pictured by images of death and destruction. The great regret and sorrow of hell are pictured by its inhabitants weeping and grinding their teeth. God's displeasure and wrath are pictured by the image of punishment. The terrible suffering and pain of hell are pictured by conscious torment and fire. Words can hardly capture its awful reality.

These images are horrible, but the reality is far worse. The words we have in Scripture are meant to warn us so we turn from the path that leads to unimaginable loss. People sometimes speak of experiences in this life being hell, but they do not yet grasp that for some the worst is yet to be.

Heaven and hell make life serious. They sober us about the present moment. But they can also awaken us to eternal possibilities. For people who trust in Jesus Christ, those possibilities include the fact that the best is yet to be.

Here's one other very important thing the Bible says about heaven. In the end, there will be a new heaven and a new earth. This is the ultimate destination of God's people. Heaven is not simply a place where disembodied souls go to be with the Lord. Though that certainly is heaven, there is more.

While we are both premillennialists when it comes to eschatology and believe in a literal millennium on this earth where Christ will come back, even this will not be heaven. In fact, in God's eyes one thousand years is not a very long time. It is a speck on the screen of history, compared to the eternal heaven. As important as this may be in the story of the Bible, the ultimate focus of Scripture is the heaven that comes after that—the new heaven and earth.

Here's what will happen. There will be a resurrection day. Following in the likeness of Christ, believers will get a new resurrection body like Jesus. There will also be a great day of judgment—a time of separation. Then He will make all things new.

The present physical universe is not eternal. The old order will end. It will be replaced by a new order (Revelation 21:1, 27; 22:3; Isaiah 65:17; 66:22; 2 Peter 3:10–13). There will be a resurrection of the cosmos, a new Genesis—the regeneration of the universe.

Scripture stretches language to describe it for us. A new

Jerusalem will come down from heaven—the dwelling place of the righteous—a restored and holy city (Revelation 21:2), a kingdom made visible (Luke 11:2), our Father's house with vacancies (John 14:2), our heavenly country (Hebrews 11:16), where God dwells with humanity, a paradise restored (2 Corinthians 12:2), where the nations walk by the light of the Lamb, where a river of the water of life flows from the throne of God, where the nations are healed, and the blessings of Eden are multiplied.

In this new world, earth will be reclaimed. In other words, this will not be an unearthly heaven. It will be very earthly, only it will be free from the curse of the broken world. It is a place where "there will be no more death or mourning or crying or pain, for the old order of things has passed away" and He will make everything pristine (Revelation 21:4–5). Think of it, no frustrations with our bodies, no deformities, bodies with new capacities—glorified bodies like Jesus' after His resurrection.

We will live in a garden temple that will make the original Eden look bland. There we will not only worship the Lord and enjoy His presence, but we will also serve Him and work with new capacities. It will be anything but boring. We will continue to learn, grow, and develop. We will oversee His world as good stewards, as we failed to do in the first. We will never exhaust exploring the Creator and His handiwork, because we will still be finite and He will still be infinite. We will explore the depths of His love, His wisdom, and His holiness. We will do this with others, but we will do it without selfishness and all the things that gum up our relationships now.

Yes, there will be a reunion of the redeemed. We will recognize others just as the disciples recognized Moses and Elijah on the Mount of Transfiguration, and just as they recognized Jesus after the tomb was empty.

We will see those again who are Christ's people whose names are written in the Lamb's Book of Life (Revelation 21:27). We will never come to the end of appreciating, exploring, and serving with them either. In this heaven, we will never say good-bye, and the circle will no longer be broken.

DO YOU KNOW YOUR HOPE?

Do you know this hope? Over the years we have met so many believers who do not know of these things. They are ignorant of what comes at the end. They approach death with paralyzing fear. They do not have the big picture. Sadly, they think, to die is loss. They do not realize that for those who are in Christ, the best is yet to be.

Get to know your hope! Don't stop reading your Bibles, because faith comes by hearing the Word (Romans 10:17).

Read some good books on heaven. Read *Heaven,* by Randy Alcorn or *One Minute after You Die,* by Erwin Lutzer. Read *Heaven Revealed,* by Paul Enns. Or read *Jonathan Edwards on Heaven and Hell,* by Owen Strachan and Douglas Sweeney. Read Joni Eareckson Tada's *Heaven: Your Real Home.* Or read *If I Should Die before I Wake: Help for Those Who Hope for Heaven*, by K. Scott Oliphint and Sinclair B. Ferguson.

To get a sense of the journey to heaven, get an up-to-date edition of that great Christian classic we have alluded to throughout this book, *Pilgrim's Progress.* Get a readable edition such as *The Pilgrim's Progress in Modern English* from Sovereign Grace Publishers.

THE BEST THING ABOUT HEAVEN

Let's end this chapter by considering the best thing about heaven. The best thing is not that we will again see our loved ones who die in the Lord, although that will be wonderful. The best thing is not that we will have resurrection bodies, though many of us can hardly wait for that. Nor is the best thing that the earth will be restored.

So what could be better than all these wonderful things? The very best thing about heaven is that we will be united with the Lord Himself, who is our life and joy. All the joys of this heaven and earth—and the next heaven and earth—wonderful as they are, are secondary joys. They pale in comparison to the joys of knowing the triune God who is our chief joy.

In Psalm 16:2, David is right when he says, Lord, "apart from you I have no good thing." Notice what else he says. He writes that "the sorrows of those will increase who run after other gods" (v. 4). This, we know, is true. Now consider the opposite. For it is also true that the joys of those will increase who run after the one true God and His Son, Jesus Christ.

These joys will be multiplied in heaven. Our hearts have capacities for joy that have not yet been tapped. But heaven will reveal how great and deep and lasting are the joys to be found in God alone.

Perhaps that is why the psalmist ends with the words, "you will fill me with joy in your presence, with eternal pleasures at your right hand" (v. 11). Eternal joy and lasting pleasures found in Him—that is the best thing about heaven.

A FINAL WORD:
"GIVE 'EM HEAVEN!"

"WHAT IS YOUR ONLY COMFORT IN LIFE AND IN
DEATH? THAT I AM NOT MY OWN, BUT BELONG—BODY
AND SOUL, IN LIFE AND IN DEATH—TO MY FAITHFUL
SAVIOR JESUS CHRIST. HE HAS FULLY PAID FOR ALL
MY SINS WITH HIS PRECIOUS BLOOD, AND HAS SET
ME FREE FROM THE TYRANNY OF THE DEVIL. HE ALSO
WATCHES OVER ME IN SUCH A WAY THAT NOT A HAIR
CAN FALL FROM MY HEAD WITHOUT THE WILL OF MY
FATHER IN HEAVEN: IN FACT, ALL THINGS MUST WORK
TOGETHER FOR MY SALVATION. BECAUSE
I BELONG TO HIM, CHRIST, BY HIS HOLY SPIRIT,
ASSURES ME OF ETERNAL LIFE AND MAKES ME
WHOLEHEARTEDLY WILLING AND READY
FROM NOW ON TO LIVE FOR HIM."[1]
— *THE HEIDELBERG CATECHISM*

IN THIS BOOK we have described the Christian life as a long-
distance journey that requires a marathon mind-set. We have re-
viewed some of the challenges and opportunities of following Christ

in the second half of life. And we have talked about the end and goal of the journey.

There are still two final things to say.

First, you're not dead yet! There is still more time to write the story of your life and build a legacy. Who knows how long you have. Is it one year? Is it five? Is it twenty? Is it forty? You do not know how many days God has numbered for you.

As long as you have today, make it count. Don't wait for some future day to start living for Christ. Do so now. You belong to Him. So, given all that He has done for you, give yourself now whole-heartedly to Him. Find the joy that is found in Christ today! Use what you have left for Christ and His kingdom. Persevere. Go the distance. By the power of the Holy Spirit, commit yourself today to live the rest of your days without regret.

Second, as you encounter the people and culture around you, "give 'em heaven." You've heard the opposite phrase. That's what many people give us. It is so easy to imitate them and do the same. But Jesus calls us to a better way. So give 'em heaven!

It was sometimes said in the past that Christians were so "heavenly minded that they were no earthly good." The story of church history has actually proved the opposite. It is only when we have perspective, when we have the big story in mind, that we are so heavenly minded that we are the most earthly good! Why? Because we know what values stand at the center of the universe and what really matters to God.

Perhaps that is why Paul exhorts that first European church, the church of Philippi, to live as a colony of heaven. The ancient city of Philippi, filled with retired Roman soldiers from the imperial capital, trying hard to be a little Rome far from Rome, knew what it was to be a colony of that great city.

So Paul appealed to the church there to do the same—to live as a colony of heaven. That's a timely word for the church today. We live under the reign of a different king—Jesus the Lord. Our ultimate allegiance is to a different kingdom—the kingdom of heaven. We are ultimately bound to the laws of our true homeland. In the meantime, we must represent that land well until the Lord comes again and the kingdoms of this world become the kingdom of the Lord and of His Christ.

As we bless others in the name of Christ, may they catch a glimpse of a better land and a more lasting kingdom. By the grace of God and the Spirit's power, may they be wooed through our lives and our corporate witness into joining us on the journey. Yes, yes . . . give 'em heaven! Give 'em heaven!

NOTES

Introduction

1. "Country Comparison: Life Expectancy at Birth," *The World Factbook*, Central Intelligence Agency. www.cia.gov/library/publications/the-world-factbook/rankorder/2102rank.html.

2. "World Population Prospects: The 2006 Revision," 14, 17. www.un.org/esa/population/publications/wpp2006/WPP2006_Highlights_rev.pdf.

3. "Richard Baxter: Moderate in an Age of Extremes," *Christian History*. www.christianitytoday.com/ch/131christians/pastorsandpreachers/baxter.html.

Chapter 1: Long-Distance Christianity

1. "John Stephen Akhwari—the greatest last place finish ever," from the official website of the Beijing 2008 Olympic Games. http://en.beijing2008.cn/education/stories/n214077658.shtml.

2. Christopher B. Swanson, "U.S. Graduation Rate Continues Decline," *Education Week*, June 2, 2010, published online. www.edweek.org/ew/articles/2010/06/10/34swanson.h29.html.

3. Paul L. Maier, *Eusebius: The Church History, A New Translation with Commentary* (Grand Rapids: Kregel, 1999), 145ff.

Chapter 2: The Gospel for the Second Half

1. "Changes in the Body with Aging," *The Merck Manual Home Health Handbook.* www.merckmanuals.com/home/older_peoples_health_issues/the_aging_body/changes_in_the_body_with_aging.html.

Chapter 3: Wisdom Insights of an Octogenarian

1. Lee Iacocca, *Where Have All the Leaders Gone?* (New York: Scribner, 2007), 244.

2. John Stott, recalled from his talk, "Lessons from Leadership: Reflections of an Octogenarian." Presented in abbreviated form in his book *The Living Church* (Downers Grove, Ill.: InterVarsity, 2007), 170.

Chapter 4: Retirement Rebels

1. Mary-Lou Weisman, "The History of Retirement, from Early Man to A.A.R.P.," *New York Times*, March 21, 1999. www.nytimes.com/1999/03/21/jobs/the-history-of-retirement-from-early-man-to-aarp.html.

2. Quotation recalled by memory from George Sweeting. See also: Billy Sunday, *The Sawdust Trail: Billy Sunday in His Own Words* (Iowa City: University of Iowa Press, 2005) and *Men Who Saw Revival: Billy Sunday.* http://menwhosawrevival.blogspot.com/p/billy-sunday.html .

3. John Piper, *Rethinking Retirement: Finishing Life for the Glory of Christ* (Wheaton: Crossway, 2009).

4. Kay Strom, *The Second-Half Adventure: Don't Just Retire—Use Your Time, Skills & Resources to Change the World* (Chicago: Moody, 2009), 41.

Chapter 5: You Can't Run This Race Alone

1. Rick Weinberg, "Derek and Dad Finish Olympic 400 Together," ESPN.com. http://sports.espn.go.com/espn/espn25/story?page=moments/94.

2. Dick Patrick, "Baton drops mar U.S. efforts in both 4x100 relays," *USA Today.* http://www.usatoday.com/sports/olympics/beijing/track/2008-08-21-sprintrelays_N.htm.

Chapter 6: Eleven Jobs and Counting

1. "Number of Jobs Held, Labor Market Activity, and Earnings Growth among the Youngest Baby Boomers," September 10, 2010. www.bls.gov/news.release/pdf/nlsoy.pdf.

2. Ibid.

3. William Orme, *Practical Works of the Rev. Richard Baxter, Vol. 2* (London: James Duncan, 1830), 332.

4. Sara Mednick and Mark Ehrman, *Take a Nap! Change Your Life* (New York: Workman Publishing, 2006), 8.
See also David E. Fisher, *A Summer Bright and Terrible: Winston Churchill, Lord Dowding, Radar, Radar, and the Impossible Triumph of the Battle of Britain* (Berkeley, Calif.: Counter Point, 2006), 233.

5. Tom Peters, *Re-Imagine: Business Excellence in a Disruptive Age* (London: DK, 2003), 243.

Chapter 7: Pacesetters

1. "Rower suffers Aussie backlash," http://news.bbc.co.uk/sport2/hi/olympics_2004/rowing/3597914.stm.

2. J. Robert Clinton, "Focused Lives Lectures," given at Lincoln Seminary, 1996 7. http://jrclintoninstitute.com/resource-store/articles/focused-lives-lectures/.

3. Billy Graham, *Just As I Am* (New York: Harper, 1997), 243.

4. Ibid., 151.

5. Ibid., 414.

6. Ibid., 40.

7. Timothy Dudley-Smith, *John Stott: The Making of a Leader: A Biography of the Early Years* (Downers Grove, Ill.: InterVarsity, 1999), quotations displayed on the cover.

8. Ibid.

9. From founding, in-house documents, and early conversations in the board meetings of John Stott Ministries.

10. Bruce L. Shelley, *Transformed by Love: The Vernon Grounds Story* (Grand Rapids: Discovery House, 2002), 228 ff.

Chapter 8: You Can't Take It with You When You Go

1. Thomas Jackson, ed., *The Works of Rev. John Wesley, Vol. 7* (London: Wesleyan Methodist Book Room, 1831. Reprinted Grand Rapids: Baker, 1978), 317.

2. Gerald Garth Johnson, *Puritan Children in Exile* (Westminster, Md.: Heritage Books, 2002), 65.

Chapter 9: Dealing with Suffering

1. C. S. Lewis, *A Grief Observed* (New York: HarperCollins, 1989), 81.

2. "Sayings of Spurgeon," *Christian History Magazine,* January 1, 1991, www.ctlibrary.com/ch/1991/issue29/2912.html.

3. Larry J. Michael, *Spurgeon on Leadership: Key Insights for Christian Leaders* (Grand Rapids: Kregel, 2010), 236.

4. Editors of *Christian History Magazine, 131 Christians Everyone Should Know* (Nashville: Holman Reference, 2000), 40.

Chapter 11: The Best Funerals We Have Ever Attended

1. Pico Iyer, "America's First Renaissance Woman: Clare Boothe Luce: 1903–1987," Monday, Oct. 19, 1987. http://www.time.com/timemagazine/article/0,9171,965754,00.html.

2. Michael Hyatt, "What Will They Say When You Are Dead?" http://michaelhyatt.com/what-will-they-say-when-you-are-dead.html.

3. Jeffrey Zaslow, "Love, Honor, Cherish and Scatter," *Wall Street Journal*, Feb. 3, 2010. http://online.wsj.com/article/SB100014240527487034229045750392807993366 38.html.

Chapter 12: What We Have Learned about Finishing Well

1. John Stott, "Lessons from Leadership: Reflections of an Octogenarian," in *The Living Church: Convictions of a Lifelong Pastor* (Downers Gorve, Ill.: IVP, 2007) appendix 3.

2. Thom S. Rainer, "A Prayer to Finish Well." www.thomrainer.com/2009/10/a-prayer-to-finish-well.php.

Chapter 13: The Somber Season

1. Susan Jacoby, *Never Say Die: The Myth and Marketing of the New Old Age* (New York: Pantheon, 2011), 1.

2. Joanne Lynn and David Adamson, "Living Well at the End of Life: Adapting Health Care to Serious Chronic Illness in Old Age," Rand Health White Paper WP-137 (2003). www.medicaring.org/whitepaper/.

3. "Statistics on Nursing Homes and Their Residents." www.therubins.com/homes/stathome.htm.

4. Alan C. Clifford, "Charles Wesley." www.igracemusic.com/hymnbook/authors/charles_wesley.html.

5. "Ronald Reagan," *Wikipedia.* http://en.wikipedia.org/wiki/Ronald_ Reagan#cite_note-257 See also: Ronald Reagan, "Letters," American Presidents.org. www.americanpresidents.org/letters/39.asp.

6. Henry K. Lee, "Disabled Man Abandoned after Flight to Oakland," *SFGate.com*, December 11, 1995. http://articles.sfgate.com/1995-12-11/news/17821281_1_paramedics-nursing-home-medical-care.

Chapter 14: Dying Well and the Blessing of a Good Death

1. Arthur G. Bennett. ed., *A Puritan Prayer from The Valley of Vision: A Collection of Puritan Prayers and Devotions* (Carlisle, Penn., Banner of Truth, 1975), 200.

2. "Clement of Alexandria," *A Dictionary of Early Christian Believers*, ed., David W. Bercot (Peabody, Mass.: Hendrickson, 1998), 427.

3. John Calvin, *Golden Booklet of the True Christian Life* (Grand Rapids: Baker, 2004), 75.

4. John Bunyan, *Pilgrim's Progress, Part 2* (Carlisle, Penn.: Banner of Truth, 1977), 377.

5. Chuck Colson, "Finishing Well: A Eulogy for Bill Bright," http://townhall.com/columnists/chuckcolson/2003/07/30/finishing_well_a_eulogy_for_bill_bright.

6. Roy B. Zuck, *The Speaker's Quote Book: Over 5,000 Illustrations and Quotations for All Occasions* (Grand Rapids: Kregel, 1997), 131.

7. Charles Haddon Spurgeon, *Spurgeon's Sermons Vol. 1* (Grand Rapids: Baker, 1999), 1:229.

8. Dennis Ngien, "Picture Christ: Martin Luther's advice on preparing to die." http://www.christianitytoday.com/ct/2007/april/34.67.html.

9. Jonathan Edwards, *The Resolutions of Jonathan Edwards (1722–1723).* http://thebridgewired.com/churchblog/wp-content/uploads/2010/02/resolutions.pdf.

10. John Stott, *Issues Facing Christians Today* (Grand Rapids: Zondervan, 2006), 377.

11. According to the Cyber Hymnal, the original words to this hymn were written in French by H. A. César Malan in 1832 (*Non, ce n'est pas mourir que d'aller vers son Dieu*). George W. Bethune translated them into English in 1847. The hymn was sung at Bethune's funeral, per his request. Bob Kauflin wrote a contemporary rendition of the song on the Sovereign Grace Music album *Come Weary Saints.*

Chapter 15: In Christ the Best Is Yet to Be

1. John M. Drescher, "Death," *Pulpit Digest*, summer 1985.

2. John Bunyan, *Pilgrim's Progress, Part 2* (Carlisle, Penn.: Banner of Truth, 1977), 377.

3. Andrew Hough, "Stephen Hawking: 'heaven is a fairy story for people afraid of the dark.'" www.telegraph.co.uk/science/stephen-hawking/8515639/Stephen-Hawking-heaven-is-a-fairy-story-for-people-afraid-of-the-dark.html.

4. Maria Shriver, *What's Heaven?* (New York: Golden Books, 1999).

5. John Calvin, *Golden Booklet of the True Christian life* (Grand Rapids: Baker, 2004), 75.

6. Warren W. Wiersbe, *The Wycliffe Handbook of Preaching and Preachers* (Chicago: Moody, 1984), 209.

A Final Word

1. *The Heidelberg Catechism.* www.crcna.org/pages/heidelberg_ intro.cfm.